Tea Shop Walks
in
The Chilterns

Jean Patefield

Published by Sigma Leisure – an imprint of
Sigma Press, 1 South Oak Lane, Wilmslow, Cheshire SK9 6AR, England.

British Library Cataloguing in Publication Data
A CIP record for this book is available from the British Library.

ISBN: 1-85058-391-9

Typesetting and Design by: Sigma Press, Wilmslow, Cheshire.

Cover picture: Hambleden Valley

Printed by: Manchester Free Press

Contents

The Walks

Summary of Walks

WALK	LOCATION	DISTANCE	TEASHOP	DESCRIPTION
1	Goring	7$^1/_2$ miles	traditional	Woods and fields, return along bank of Thames. Good views. Two climbs.
2	Nuney Green & Goring Heath	2 miles	traditional	Mainly in superb beechwoods, no climbs.
3	Henley & Greys Court	5$^1/_2$ miles	stately home	Fields and woods, excellent views on return. Two climbs.
4	Fawley	3$^1/_2$ miles	garden centre	Woods and fields, one climb.
5	Hambleden & Henley	6 miles	traditional - over teddy bear shop	Along bank of Thames, return through woods and fields. One climb.
6	Hurley & Marlow	5 miles	traditional	Along banks of Thames. Explores Marlow.
7	Hambleden Valley	6 miles	restaurant and pub	Superb walk around head of beautiful Chiltern valley. Two climbs.
8	Chisbridge Cross & Booker	5 miles	traditional within garden centre	Woods and fields. Very quiet paths. Several short climbs.

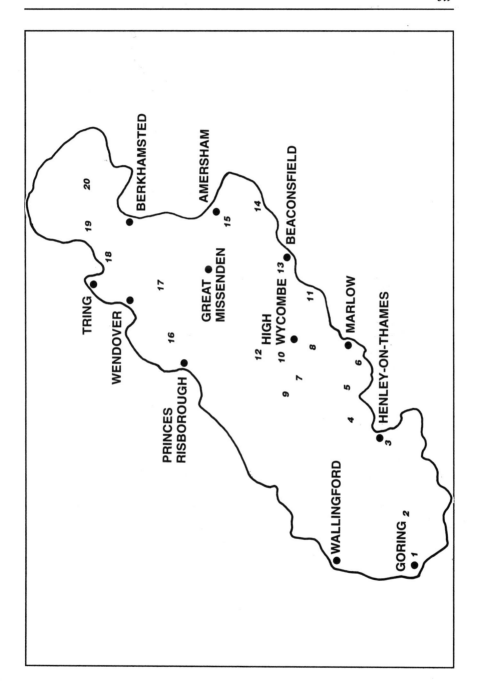

The Chilterns

The Chilterns are a range of chalk hills stretching in an arc about forty miles north and west of London. This description is accurate but conveys nothing of the paradise they are for walkers. Within the four hundred square miles encompassed by the Chilterns are about 1,500 miles of public footpaths, mostly very quiet, well signed and lovingly maintained.

The hills are not very high, about 800 feet at most, but nowhere else can such magnificent views be had for so little effort. The Chilterns were formed about twenty six million years ago as the result of a collision of truly epic proportions. The continental plate on which Africa rides crashed into the continental plate of Europe causing buckles and folds across Europe. The Alps are the most dramatic result but the same impact produced the Chilterns. To the north and west the scarp slope rises sharply and dramatically from the fertile Vale of Aylesbury while to the south and east the dip slope falls away gently to the river Thames. The western and eastern limits of the Chilterns are not so easy to define but are generally taken to be from Goring in the south-west to Ivinghoe Beacon in the north-east.

The Chilterns are essentially made of chalk; indeed the word Chiltern comes from the Saxon word for chalk. This is the cause of so many of the features typical of the Chilterns. Chalk is a very porous rock and water drains through it rapidly. Therefore the Chilterns are very dry with little running water. The rivers which do exist such as the Chess and the Misbourne are small, pathetic things compared with rivers in areas of less permeable geology. However, the walker in the Chilterns is not totally deprived of river scenery since the southern boundary is one of England's great rivers, the Thames.

Much of the charm of the Chiltern landscape comes from the valleys, nearly all dry and locally called *bottoms*. These were formed in the Ice Age. The Chilterns were not covered by ice but were frozen much of the time. During the short sub-arctic summer water flowed from the glaciers only a short distance north and eroded the valleys we see today.

If the Chilterns were just chalk they would resemble the other areas of chalk upland in southern England. However, the tops of the Chilterns are overlaid in many places with clay which is much less permeable to water and supports quite a different flora and fauna. This gives the Chilterns their great variety which contributes so much to their interest and appeal.

The glory of the Chilterns is undoubtedly the beechwoods for which they are famous: majestic without leaves in Winter, carpeted with bluebells in Spring, luminous green in Summer and brilliantly aflame in Autumn. The woods are not composed solely of beech, of course. Oak is common along with many other species.

The beechwoods are so dominant in the Chilterns due to the demands of the furniture industry, centred in High Wycombe. By the seventeenth century, the woodlands in much of southern England had been cleared but the Chilterns were still heavily wooded. They became important as a source of firewood for London and large amounts were sent by river through ports such as Henley and Marlow. As coal replaced wood as a fuel, the furniture industry grew in importance and so the demand for wood continued. Craftsmen known as bodgers moved from place to place in the woods making the parts for chairs. Until the last war, it was possible for a solitary bodger to build his bothy in the woods and set up his equipment. Most of the bodgers were entrepreneurs as well as craftsmen and bought small stands of woodland which they felled or coppiced and worked on the spot into parts for the Windsor chairs, for which the area was famous. These parts were then sold to framers who put them together ready for the polishers. Bodgers worked all along the Chiltern ridge and High Wycombe chairmasters would go out with wagons to the villages to buy the parts. The demand was huge and contemporary accounts speak of piles of chair legs seasoning in stacks outside the cottages in villages like Lane End and Turville. Their system of managing the woods (known as the Chiltern selection system) produced the magnificent beech woods we see today.

It is the landscape of the Chilterns, designated as an Area of Outstanding Natural Beauty, which attracts the walker but throughout the area are market towns and villages of great antiquity and interest. Many of the villages such as Turville, Aldbury and Hambleden are gems of English vernacular architecture in perfect settings while many of the market and coaching towns such as Wendover and Old Amersham have a great sense of place and are fascinating to explore. Tea shops are frequently found in towns and villages and so most of the walks described in this book visit an interesting old town or village.

Situated so conveniently between London and Oxford, the district has been favoured by both Church and State. There are many great estates such as Cliveden, Stonor and West Wycombe and, up to the Dissolution, monasteries abounded. Despite this, the Chilterns were well known as a hotbed of dissent and defiance of authority. Chiltern people were prominent in the Lollard rising of 1413 – 14 and later, in the sixteenth century, dissenters were burned at the stake in Amersham. The Quakers, often imprisoned for their refusal to accept the established church, also flourished in the Chilterns.

The Chilterns were once the Wild West! In the Middle Ages the area was poor and thickly wooded. As such it became notorious for thieves and highwaymen who preyed on travellers using the important routes to Oxford and the North and on the Icknield Way making pilgrimage to Lincoln Cathedral. Hundreds were once administrative districts and the Steward of the Chiltern Hundred was appointed to control these depredations by the lawless Chiltern residents.

Many people have heard of the Chilterns because the post of Steward of the Chiltern Hundreds has been retained as a political device to the present day. An MP may not resign but neither may he or she hold a civil office for profit. The convention is that to resign, an M.P. applies for the Stewardship of the Chiltern Hundred and then immediately gives it up so that it is vacant for the next M.P. who wants to resign.

The Ridgeway

The Ridgeway is one of the great trade routes of England. It has probably been in use for four thousand years and is one of the oldest roads in the world. It runs from the Dorset coast to the North Sea and rides along the back of one of the six great ridges that radiate from Salisbury Plain. It is thought that this ancient route followed the high chalk land to avoid the thick forests and marshes and prehistoric remains are found in abundance along its length.

Keeping company with the Ridgeway for some of its length is another ancient highway, the Icknield Way, though it came into being later than the Ridgeway. The Ridgeway, being on top of chalk hills, had no water suppy, which is why there are no villages on it today. The Icknield Way runs nearer to the spring line so giving travellers easier access to water. It came into use later when, presumably, there were fewer dangers from wolves and other wild animals in the woods. It is still very old and has an older name than the Ridgeway. The Ridgeway is what its name implies in modern English and gets its name from the Anglo-Saxon "hryeg" meaning ridge. Icknield is a name so old it has no known root and must embody some word from a long forgotten tongue. The Icknield Way divides into the Upper and Lower Icknield Way for part of its length. The Upper Way is above the spring line and must have provided a drier route in wet weather. The Lower Way is now a road and has many villages along it but the Upper Way is still mainly track. The Ridgeway and Icknield Way were already ancient when the Romans came. They ignored the Ridgeway, it was too high and dry for them, but they used stretches of the Icknield Way.

The Ridgeway Path is a modern creation. It was proposed by the Ramblers association in 1942 and brought into being by the Countryside Commission as one of the long distance routes. The long distance path runs from Ivinghoe Beacon in Buckinghamshire to Overton Hill in Wiltshire. In part it runs along the ancient Ridgeway but also uses other paths. In the Chilterns it runs mainly along the top of the scarp slope and gives wonderful views out across the Vale of Aylesbury. Several of the walks in this book make use of this well-known path; see the summary chart at the end of the contents pages of this book.

The Chiltern Society

The Chiltern Society was founded in 1965 and aims to sustain the beauty and character of the Chilterns and to conserve and enhance their rich heritage of ecological, archaeological and architectural features. It does sterling work protecting the Chilterns and in the context of this book, the Rights of Way Group is invaluable in actively protecting and maintaining rights of way. They monitor the state of footpaths and bridleways and take up problems with landowners and local authorities. They are also responsible for the white arrows that mark public rights of way and do practical work such as path clearance and repairing stiles.

Details of membership and activities can be obtained from the Assistant General Secretary, The Chiltern Society, 27 Chalfont Road, Maple Cross, Rickmansworth WD3 2TA.

TEA SHOPS

Afternoon Tea is often said to be the best meal to eat out in England: scones with cream and strawberry jam, delicious home made cakes, toasted tea cakes dripping with butter in winter, delicate cucumber sandwiches in summer all washed down with the cup that cheers! Bad for the figure maybe, but the walking will see to that.

Tea shops are such an English institution and what could be more appropriate during a walk in such English countryside than refreshment at a tea shop. The best tea shops offer a range of cakes, all home made and including fruit cake as well as scones and other temptations. Cream teas should, of course, feature clotted cream. Tea pots should be capacious and pour properly. Ideally, there should be a attractive garden where tea can be taken outside in summer. Many of the tea shops visited on these walks fulfil all these criteria admirably.

However, the Chilterns for all their beauty and accessibility, are not a well known tourist area and there are not as many traditional tea shops as in some other areas. Therefore a few of the tea shops visited on the walks in this book are in unusual places such as garden centres and stately homes. However, they all offer a good afternoon tea part-way round an attractive walk.

The Walks

The twenty walks in this book are all between 2 and $7^1/_2$ miles and should be within the capacity of the average person. They are intended to take the walker through some of the loveliest scenery in Southern England at a gentle pace with plenty of time to stop and stare, and to savour the beauty and interest all around. A dedicated yomper and stomper could probably knock off the whole book in a single weekend but, in doing so, they would have missed the point and seen nothing. To fully appreciate the countryside it is necessary to go slowly with your eyes and ears open.

The Chilterns are not high hills but there is an occasional steep ascent. However, they present no problem to the sensible walker who has three uphill gears – slowly, very slowly and stopping and staring. In some places in winter after rain the mud can be ferocious and is particularly bad on any paths which happen to be bridleways and churned up by horses. Where an alternative path is available, it is suggested. At such times, wellies or boots are very welcome. At other times fairly stout shoes are all that is required.

All the routes are on public rights of way or permissive paths and have been carefully checked but, of course, in the countryside things do change; a gate is replaced by a stile or a wood is extended. In the Chilterns the footpaths are guarded by the Chiltern Society and nearly always marked by white or occasionally yellow or blue arrows. In certain areas where there is unrestricted public access such as Ashridge or Naphill Common there are many other, unmarked paths and careful attention should be paid to the directions.

Each walk is illustrated by a map. All the walks are circular with one exception: the walk between Great Missenden and Wendover is an exhilarating ridge walk and uses the frequent train service to return to the starting point. The walks are all designed so that, starting where suggested, the tea shop is reached in the second half so a really good appetite can be worked up.

The starting point of some walks can be reached easily by public transport. Most of the others can be reached by public transport if the route is modified slightly to start in a different place.

1. Goring

Route: This walk is the longest one in the book, but is worth the effort for its excellent views. There are a few climbs but nothing too strenuous. The route starts on the outskirts of Whitchurch and goes to Goring through typical Chiltern scenery of woods and fields. It returns along the banks of the Thames and includes the lovely Goring Gap.

Tea shop: The Riverside Tea Room is, as the name implies, very close to the Thames in Goring. It is open every day from 9.15am until 5.30pm except during January, February and March when it closes completely. There are some tables outside. Usually there is a wide variety of cakes available as well as the usual scones and tea-cakes.
Tel: 0491 872243

Distance: $7^1/_2$ miles.

Map: OS Landranger 175 Reading and Windsor.

How to get there: The walk starts on the B471 which goes from the A4074 Wallingford – Reading road to Pangbourne on the A329 Reading – Wantage road.

Start: $1/_2$ mile north of Whitchurch. There is space to park on a rough layby by the War Memorial and the entrance to Stoneycroft. From the north this is on the right as you are driving downhill immediately after a left-hand bend.
SU 634780

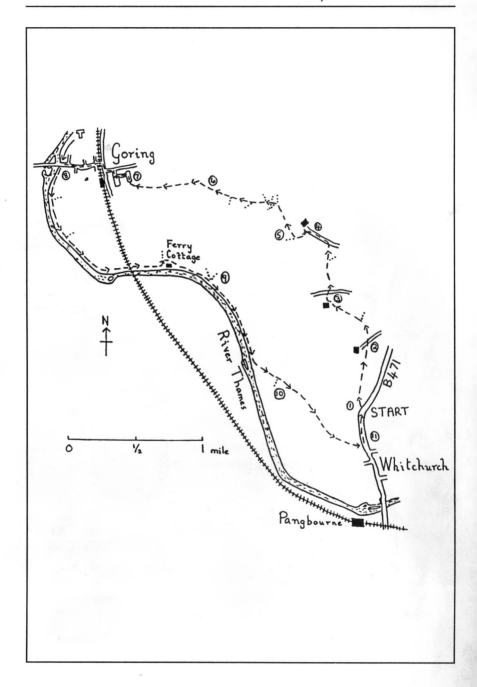

1. Just beyond the entrance to Stoneycroft take a narrow unsigned path uphill. Bear left to a metal kissing gate and continue along the left-hand side of the field. At the far end go through another kissing gate and follow the path between fences to a farm.

2. Cross the farm drive and continue ahead on a signed path towards a wood. Follow the path as it winds through the wood. Towards the far end of the wood take the left fork out of the wood. After the stile out of the wood the path is not visible on the ground but goes across two fields toward the right-hand side of some farm buildings. Do not go through the gate but take a stile on the right and turn left to walk round the left-hand side of the field to a stile by a gate.

3. Turn right along the farm track. Cross the lane and continue on a farm drive on the other side. Stay on this to a T-junction with a surfaced drive and then turn left.

4. The drive ends at a farm. 50 yards before the farm go through a metal gate on the left and walk over to a gate in the far right-hand corner of the field which leads on to a sunken track. Follow this downhill.

5. 20 yards after a gate turn right on a clear path marked by blue arrows on trees. Follow the main path as it makes a pronoun-ced left bend, ignoring a path continuing in the same direction through a gate. The arrows on the trees are now yellow. Ignore a path on the left after 50 yards and stay on the path marked by yellow arrows ignoring all side turns and cross paths for $1/2$ mile to a stile out of the wood.

6. Follow the path along the right-hand side of the field and then turn left along the top of the field. At the far end cross a stile and continue along the top of a second field. Goring can be seen below. Go through a hedge gap and take a stile on the right onto a playing field. Go across or round – depending on the state of play – to a stile on the far side.

7. At the end of a short hedged path join a road on an estate of large, modern houses. Follow the road round to the left and turn right at a T-junction. At the next T-junction turn left. Turn right at the Queens Arms and then left over the railway. Follow this road down into Goring. The tea shop is on the right past the shops just before the river.

Goring, like the other Thames side towns of Henley and Marlow, is an ancient settlement. Streatley is its twin across the river and in modern times, with the bridge, they are one place. At one time the two towns were linked by a ferry and ford. In 1674 a ferry capsized and all sixty people on board were drowned. On the other hand, Goring seems good for your health. In the church is a memorial to one Hugh Whistler who died in 1615 aged 216!

The Miller of Mansfield Inn is a mixture of three buildings – a seventeenth century brick and flint wing, the main block is Georgian and there are Victorian additions. It is a very popular resting place with people walking the Ridgeway which crosses the Thames here. The name is supposed to derive from an early inn keeper who came from Sherwood Forest. King Henry II was out hunting and became separated from his party. He begged a bed and meal from a miller who had no idea of his guests identity. His wife served what she called a "lightfoot pastry" and the King remarked that it tasted like venison which of course it couldn't be since all deer belonged to the King and poaching them was such a serious offence. The miller said that what the King didn't know wouldn't harm him and that he had several carcases in the roof. The next day the rest of the hunting party found the King and the miller saw the noose beckon. However, the King was so grateful for the miller's generosity that he let him off providing he continued to provide hospitality to weary travellers. It makes a good story anyway!

8. From the tea shop cross the road and take the path to the river. Turn left along the river bank. After about a mile the path goes under a railway bridge. In another $^1/_4$ mile the path is temporarily forced away from the river bank at Ferry Cottage. Turn left and go over a small wooden bridge. Turn right

immediately and the path soon comes back to the river bank. The next $1/4$ mile can be rather overgrown and infested with nettles. The path then climbs up a short distance to a path junction.

You are now walking through Goring Gap, one of the loveliest stretches of the river, where the Thames breaks through the chalk hills.

9. Turn right and continue with the river on the right, now climbing steadily through a wood. Eventually the path veers away from the river. It drops into a dip and there are some steps to help you up the steep climb on the other side.

Below: Goring Lock

10. At the top it joins the track to Hartslock Farm. Go ahead along the track in the same direction for $^3/_4$ mile to a road.

11. Turn left for $^1/_4$ mile back to the starting place. There is a good path on the right-hand side of the road.

2. Nuney Green and Goring Heath

Route: This is a walk between two hamlets, mainly through beechwoods. It is particularly recommended as a winter walk since the tea shop has an open fire where you can toast your muffins but it is beautiful at any time of year.

Tea shop: The tea shop is in Goring Heath Post Office which is no longer used as a post office. It is particularly attractive in winter with its open fire and in the summer there is a very pleasant garden. They sell a wide variety of excellent homemade cakes and have pleasingly capacious tea pots. It is open every day Tuesday to Saturday from 9am to 6pm and Sundays and Bank Holidays from 10am to 6pm.
Tel: 0491 680200

Distance: 2 miles.

Map: Landranger OS 175 Reading and Windsor.

How to get there: From the A4074 Reading – Wallingford road take a minor road signed Mapledurham, Trench Green and Mapledurham Mill. After 2 miles turn right on a very minor road signed Nuney Green only.

Start: Where the surfaced road ends. There are a few places it is possible to pull safely off the road or down the track to the left.
SU 672792

1. Where the surfaced road ends at a T-junction with a track, turn
left along the track. When the track ends continue along an
unsigned path in the same direction to the left of a thatched
cottage called Straw Eaves. Follow the path as it winds through
the woods. It is marked by occasional white arrows on trees. It
skirts to the right of a pond and at this point be sure to follow
the marked path and ignore unmarked paths right and left.

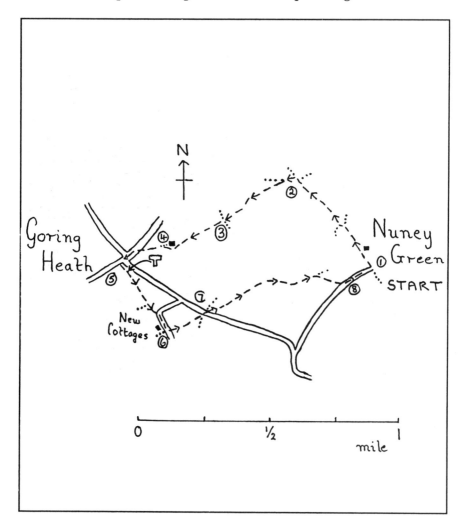

2. After another $1/4$ mile the wood on the right ends and there is a field and open views on the right. At this point a path joins on the right and in 20 yards take a path on the left. This is all marked by arrows on trees. After 100 yards bear left at a fork and follow the marked path through the wood to a stile.

3. Over the stile the path is not visible on the ground. Head across the field towards some farm buildings and then go a few yards left to a stile. Continue along the right-hand side of a field to a stile onto a track.

Woods near Goring Heath

4. Turn left. At a road turn left again to Goring Heath Post Office and Tea Room in 100 yards.

Goring on the Thames (about 4 miles away and visited on walk 1) and Goring Heath are typical of many Chiltern parishes. They used to be very long and thin stretching from the base of the hills up to the top. This meant that each covered the full range of farming possibilities. Reorganisations of local government have subsequently split them up into separate parts. Goring Heath today is a scattered hamlet. The tea shop is in the delightful post office built in 1900.

5. On leaving the tea shop take an signed bridleway next to it which passes down the side of the garden between hedges. The path joins a track. Continue along the track in the same direction to a lane. Turn right.

6. 5 yards after New Cottages on the right turn left over a stile. The path is not apparent on the ground but goes along the left-hand side of two fields to a road.

7. Go straight across the road and take the public footpath directly opposite. The path forks immediately. Take the right fork which is marked by white arrows on trees. Follow this path through the wood, ignoring all side paths and following the white arrows. Shortly after a sharp ascent the path forks. Take the right fork, shown by the usual white arrows.

8. When the path ends at a lane turn left along the lane back to the starting point.

3. Henley to Greys Court

Route: This is one of the best short walks from Henley. The route is fairly level and returns through Lambridge Wood.

Tea shop: Greys Court is a property owned by the National Trust in a beautiful setting with lovely gardens and a tea shop. The gardens are open every day except Thursday and Sunday from 2pm to 6pm from April to the end of September. The House is only open on Monday, Wednesday and Friday.
Tel: 0491 628529

Distance: $5^1/_2$ miles.

Map: Landranger OS 175 Reading and Windsor.

How to get there: The walk starts and finishes in Henley, where there are numerous car parks. Alternatively, Henley can be reached by train from London Paddington and Reading or by bus from London, Oxford and Reading.

Start: The directions are given from the traffic lights in the middle of the town at the junction of Bell Street, Market Place, Hart Street and Duke Street.
SU 761826

Henley is a very interesting town to explore. It is said to be the oldest town in Oxfordshire. The name is Saxon and means "high enclosure or clearing". Its position on the Thames and the road to London has always been important. Apart from malting, Henley had no real industries but was an important riverside port trading in timber, corn and malt. In the eighteenth century the town became a coaching stop between London and Oxford and there was much rebuilding and refronting of houses at this period. The railway arrived in 1857 and there has been further expansion since. Henley has over three hundred listed buildings of many styles and periods. The Kenton Theatre in New Street was built in 1805 and is one of the oldest theatres in the country still in use. The Bull Inn in Bell Street is the oldest pub in Henley dating in part from 1326. It serves very good bar meals.

1. From the traffic lights walk along Duke Street and at the next junction turn right along Greys Road.

2. Turn right into Deanfield Road and turn immediately left along a track by Henley Youth Centre. This soon becomes a path and continue ahead to emerge at a road.

3. Turn left and then turn right down Tilebarn Close. Bear left in front of a small car park to continue on the path to the left of some playing fields.

4. Cross a track and take the left fork immediately to continue along the bottom of the valley.

5. At the end of the first field the path goes over a stile a few yards uphill and continues over a further stile to join a track from a farm. When the wood on the right ends at a cross tracks, carry on in the same direction across a field.

6. When the track bears left and uphill take a path over a stile on the right and follow the path along the left-hand side of three fields, ignoring paths to the right and left. Do NOT take the stile into the wood on the left but skirt round the wood and pass a house on the left. There is a good view of Grey's Court ahead and right.

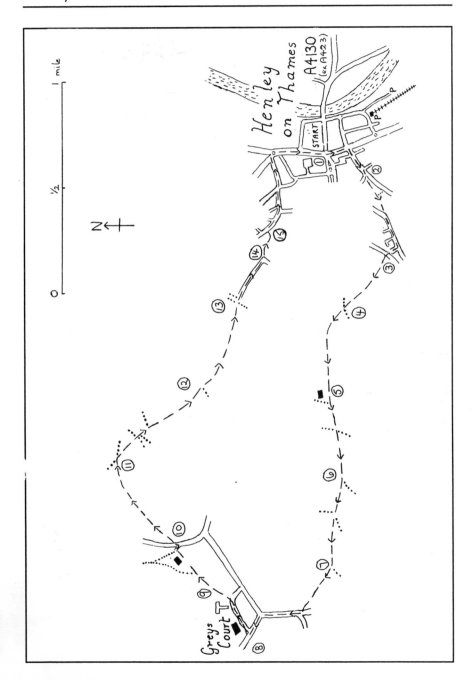

7. The path comes to another stile into a wood. Cross this and follow the path up to a minor road. Turn right and then right again at the more major road in 20 yards.

8. After 300 yards where the road bends right, take the lane on the left. 30 yards after the drive on the right, take a public footpath which goes over a stile after 10 yards and then soon joins the drive which leads to the house and gardens.

Greys Court was originally a castle built by one Walter de Grey in the fourteenth century. The very deep well and a donkey wheel for drawing water are still to be seen. Three towers and part of the walls remain as a romantic backdrop to the gardens. Within the defence the Knollys family built their Elizabethan mansion which, of course, has been added to and altered many times since.

Greys Court

9. To continue the walk return to the drive and turn left to walk up to the entrance kiosk where the drive bends right. Leave the drive and continue in the same direction across a field used as a car park to a stile and follow a marked path. Ignore the left turn a few yards after a pond and continue to a stile by some farm buildings. Cross the stile and turn right to follow the path between a wire fence and a line of beech trees to a lane.

10. Turn right and then left at a T-junction. After 15 yards turn right on a signed path going diagonally into a wood. Follow the path marked by yellow arrows through lovely beechwoods for $1/2$ mile ignoring all side turns and cross paths.

11. At a cross paths with both paths shown by yellow arrows on a beech tree turn right to follow path 48. This path is also marked through the wood by yellow arrows. After 200 yards there is a poorly signed complicated junction with path 50. Take the path that goes gently downhill with a field on the right. After 100 yards path 50 leaves path 48 over a stile on the right. Continue on path 48 through the wood, following the yellow arrows.

12. As the wood comes to an end, watch for a metal barn on the right. Level with this is a beech tree showing, rather faintly, a junction of paths 48 and 49. Follow the direction shown for path 48, slightly left, to a golf course. Follow the path in the same direction across the golf course following a line of trees. This gradually becomes a better-defined track.

13. When the track turns right towards the club house, take the stile ahead by the white iron gate onto a track. Turn right. The track soon becomes a minor road.

14. After $1/4$ mile it makes a sharp bend right and there is a public footpath on the left. This goes downhill into Henley.

15.Turn right at the road down hill. At the T-junction turn right
   and then first left into Badgemore Lane. At the main road turn
   right and at the roundabout turn right again. This is Bell Street
   which leads back to the starting point.

4. Fawley

Route: This walk starts in Fawley village and goes down to the Thames at Fawley Court. It returns via Rowe Wood and Benhams.

Tea shop: This is in Toad Hall Garden Centre by Fawley Court. It is a very pleasant place to stop with sensible tea pots and has tables both inside and out. It is open 10.30am to 4.30pm in the winter and until 5pm in summer. Tel: 0491 574615

Distance: $3^1/_2$ miles.

Map: Landranger OS 175 Reading and Windsor.

How to get there: From the A4155 Henley to Marlow road 2 miles north of Henley take a minor road signed Fawley 1. Coming from Henley, this is the second road signed Fawley. At the T-junction turn left to the church.

Start: From St. Mary the Virgin church in Fawley. There is adequate parking by the church. SU 753867

Fawley is a scattered hilltop village. There has been a church on this site for 800 years. The earliest parts of the present building date from the late twelfth or early thirteenth centuries. It was substantially altered in 1748 by the then Lord of the manor, Lord Freeman and then remodelled again in the Victorian era. In modern times there has been an attempt to restore the earlier Georgian character.

The most unusual features of Fawley church are the mausoleums in the church yard. The one at the rear of the churchyard is the Freeman mausoleum designed by John Freeman in 1750 and loosely based on the tomb of Caecilia Metella in Rome. The one by the lych gate is that of William Dalziel Mackenzie who bought the Fawley estate in 1853 and died in 1863.

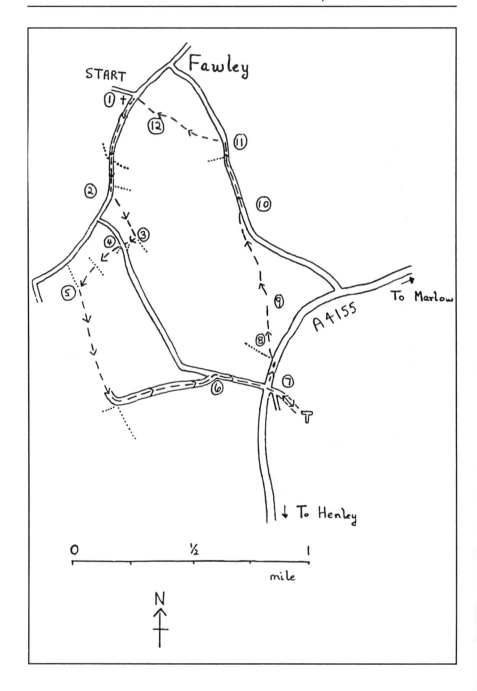

1. From the church turn right along the lane for $^1/_2$ a mile, ignoring paths left and right after $^1/_4$ mile.

2. When the lane bends sharply right take a signed public footpath down a track on the left.

3. 40 yards after the entrance to Homer House turn right on a signed public footpath. Do not bear left into the wood but continue along the edge of the wood to a lane.

4. Cross the lane and immediately bear right to cross a stile into a field. Continue ahead on the left-hand side of the field with the wood on your left to a further stile and then continue in the same direction, down into a dip and up the other side to a stile in the left-hand corner of the field. Cross the track to a stile on the other side and continue along the right-hand side of the field to a stile.

5. Turn left along the track and continue as it becomes a surfaced drive bearing left after Henley Park to follow it downhill.

6. At the minor road turn right to the A4155. Toad Hall Garden Centre is just across the road.

    Toad Hall Garden Centre is in the grounds of Fawley Court which cannot be seen from this walk. See Walk 5 page 32.

7. Retrace your steps to the A4155 and turn right for 300 yards to a stile on the left.

8. Almost immediately branch half right on a path towards the wood. At certain times of the year this path may not be visible on the ground. It goes towards the top right-hand corner of the field.

9. Cross the stile in the metal fence and follow the path through the wood to a stile onto a lane. The path is well marked by white arrows on trees.

10. Turn left. Do NOT take the first path on the left by a letter box but continue for another 100 yards to another path on the left.

11. Cross the stile and follow the path along the left-hand side of the field to a stile at the far side and continue in the same direction along a hedged path.

The field on the right often contains some animals rarely seen in the English countryside – llamas!

Llamas near Fawley

12. Go through the gate and continue along the left-hand side of the field to a gate on to a short track to the road. Turn left back to the church.

5. Hambleden and Henley

Route: This route goes from a charming and historic Chiltern village along one of the most famous stretches of the River Thames – the regatta course – to Henley and returns over the hills and by the picture postcard Hambleden lock and Mill.

Tea shop: Asquith's Tea Rooms in Henley are above a teddy bear shop (!) in a mid fifteenth century building. Throughout its long history the building has served a variety of uses including a bicycle shop (as shown in a picture in the Mayor's parlour) and the residence of the Brazilian ambassador in the Second World War. This is the classic tea shop serving a variety of excellent cakes and scones which they claim are the best in England! It is open from 9am to 6pm including Sunday.
Tel: 0491 571978

Distance: 6 miles.

Map: Landranger OS 175 Reading and Windsor.

How to get there: 3 miles from Henley or five miles from Marlow on the A4155 Henley – Marlow road turn up the road signed Hambleden 1. Turn right into Hambleden village on a road signed Pheasants Hill, Frieth and Lane End.

Start: Public car park in Hambleden next to the Stag and Huntsman.
SU 785866

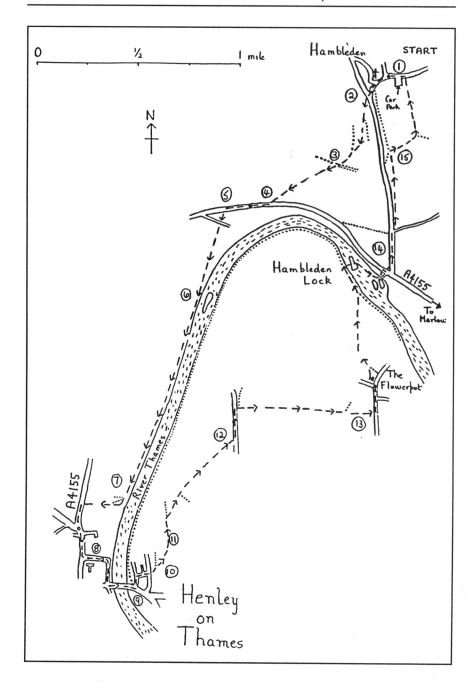

1. Walk back through the village to the road you were on before turning into Hambleden, ignoring the footpath by the bridge.

Hambleden is a picturesque village with a remarkable amount of history for such a small place.

The church of St. Mary is worth a visit even by those not usually interested in such things. The church was first built in Saxon times but the font is probably the only survivor from that date. The church we see today is Norman though there has been much rebuilding and restoring down the ages. The Norman tower collapsed in 1703 and the present one was built eighteen years later. The monuments include one to Sir Cope D'Oyley, his wife and their ten children. The children shown holding skulls died before their parents. The inscription detailing the virtues of Lady D'Oyley is said to be by her brother, Francis Quarles, Poet Laureate and is particularly fine though it is too long to quote here.

The oak altar in the south transept is an excellent example of early sixteenth century carving and includes the arms of Cardinal Wolsey and Bishop Fox. The panelling was once a bed head believed to belong to the Sandys family of the Vyne where Wolsey was a frequent visitor. The panelling came to Hambleden through the marriage of a member of the family to a Scrope, long time lords of the manor.

Hambleden has three famous sons. Thomas de Cantilupe was Chancellor of England and Bishop of Hereford. He was the last pre-reformation English saint and was born at the manor house in 1218. The church used to contain some of his relics. Adrian Scrope, who was one of the signatories of the death warrant of Charles I, came from Hambleden as did Lord Cardigan who led the Light Brigade into the "Valley of Death". A famous adopted son was W.H. Smith, the stationer who was satirised by Gilbert and Sullivan in HMS Pinafore because "he never went to sea and rose to be Ruler of the Queen's Navee". He is buried in the church yard.

In 1315 Hambleden was granted a charter from Edward II to hold a fair. It was revived in 1864 and 1955 to raise money for the church and school. It was held on Mid-Summer's eve and discontinued a few years after its last revival because of rowdy behaviour.

2. Cross the road and take the public footpath opposite. When the path forks take the right-hand branch, continuing upwards. Just over the brow on the hill, ignore a path on the right and continue ahead downhill.

3. At a T-junction turn right for 5 yards and then left to join a path leading to a wooden gate into a field. The path in the field is not visible on the ground: it goes down the left-hand side of the field, across a stile and diagonally right across a second field to a gate onto a main road.

4. Turn right along the road for ¹/₄ of a mile.

5. Cross a stile on the left and follow the path across a field crossing the drive to Henley Management College and bridges over streams to the bank of the Thames.

6. Follow the path along the bank of the Thames for 1 mile.

The stately home passed on the right is Fawley Court, formerly the home of the Freeman family. They built most of Fawley village, the start of walk 4. The house is now a Catholic College. Temple Island had a white "temple" built in 1771 as a vista for Fawley Court and is the start of the regatta course.

The stretch of river you are now walking beside is the famous Henley regatta course. Henley Royal Regatta is a great rowing festival, and social occasion, which has made Henley famous throughout the world. It had its origin in the first University Boat Race in June 1829. After that race the people of Henley realised that they had one of the finest stretches of river for racing in the world. In 1839 a public meeting was held in the Town Hall, attended by the local landed gentry and prominent townspeople. It was decided to establish a regatta with the aims of "producing most beneficial effects to the town" and being "a source of amusement and gratification to the neighbourhood."

The first regatta took place on 14th June 1839 with four races being held between 4pm and 7pm. It has now grown to five days of racing held in the first week of July with over 350 entries from all over the world. The Royal part of its title originated in 1861 when Prince Albert became its patron.

7. When the path along the river bank finishes at a fence go through a metal kissing gate on the right and follow the path up to the road. Turn left and then bear left at the roundabout along the main road into Henley. The tea shop is about 200 yards ahead on the corner of New Road, the first road on the left.

For more information on Henley see walk 3, page 19.

8. Walk down New Road back towards the river and turn right along the river bank. Cross the river by the bridge.

Some sort of bridge has existed in Henley for a very long time. In the sixteenth century it is known to have been a wooden bridge with a chapel dedicated to St. Anne on the bridge itself. In 1642, it was destroyed by either Parliamentary or Royalist forces and was not repaired until 1670. Whether or not the repairs were adequate, it was declared dangerous in 1754 and swept away in a great flood in 1774. The present bridge was built in 1786 to the design of William Hayward of Shrewsbury. He died before it was completed and is buried in the chancel of the parish church. There are two carved heads on the keystones. The one facing upstream represents Isis and that downstream represents Father Thames.

9. At the far side of the bridge turn left and take the path which bears right. In a few yards go through double metal gates and turn right to a gap in the hedge to the right of another set of

metal gates. Cross the lane and continue in the same direction on a signed public footpath.

10. At the far side of the field do NOT take the obvious track on the left but go through a gap in the hedge and then bear half left across the field towards a wood. As you enter the wood look on the ground on the left for the memorial to Minty, a much-loved dog.

11. Cross the stile and bear diagonally left gently uphill. When a wooden fence starts on the left take a clear branch on the right which continues uphill. At the brow of the hill ignore a path on the right and continue on the same path, now downhill. On leaving the wood carry on the same path, now gently rising again.

12. At the lane turn left for 250 yards to a stile by metal gates on the right. Follow the track ahead. When the track bends left continue in the same direction on a signed footpath across a field to a lane.

13. Turn left to The Flowerpot pub. At The Flowerpot turn left and then right in just over 50 yards on a track signed public footpath to the river. Cross the river at the lock and follow the path across the weir and to the road.

Hambleden lock with its white, weather-boarded mill is very picturesque and much photographed. The lock was enlarged in the winter of 1993/94. Hambleden lock was identified as one of five bottleneck locks where the worst overcrowding takes place. These will all be enlarged with Hambleden first. It was chosen because it is the narrowest lock below Oxford on one of the busiest stretches of the Thames. It was also in need of major maintenance work as it was previously "modernised" over 100 years ago and had reached the end of its safe operating life.

The mill originally dates from 1388. The present building is sixteenth century and was working until 1958. The building is now converted into flats.

Hambledon Mill

14. Turn right and then left in 25 yards up the road signed Hambleden, Skirmett and Fingest. After $^1/_4$ mile there is a road on the right. Take a signed public footpath into a field at this point. Follow the path parallel with the road to the far side of the field.

In 1812 the remains of a Roman farmstead were excavated in a field just by the car park ahead. The finds used to be kept in a small museum in Hambleden but have now been removed to a museum in Aylesbury where they are displayed together with photographs of the site.

15. Turn right on the crossing track. 50 yards after a barn turn left on a track signed public footpath. This finishes at a drive. Turn left for a few yards back to the car park.

6. Hurley and Marlow

Route: This walk follows the Thames from the ancient village
of Hurley along one of its most interesting sections to
Marlow. After exploring Marlow it returns by a different route.

Tea shop: Burgers have a traditional English tea shop behind a
Swiss patisserie. The cakes are delicious and laid out
temptingly on a side table. Alternatively, you can
choose something from the patisserie to have with
your tea. Cream teas are also served.
Tel: 0628 483389

Distance: 5 miles.

Map: Landranger OS 175 Reading and Windsor.

How to get there: From the A4130 4 miles east of Henley take a
signed road into Hurley village. This is the High
Street. After $1/2$ mile bear left to a car park at the end
of the road near the church.
(Note: the A4130 was the A423 until recently and is
shown thus on many maps.)

Start: From the car park in Hurley.
SU 826841

*Hurley is a very ancient village. It is mentioned in Saxon chronicles
when it lay on an important ford across the Thames. The first church,
built about 700 AD, may have been knocked about a bit by the
marauding Danes. After the Norman conquest William I confiscated
all the land and gave them to his trusted supporter Geoffrey de
Mandeville. He built a Priory here which became very wealthy over*

the following centuries and of which there are still many remains. After the Dissolution of the Monasteries the Priory Estate was acquired by the Lovelace family for £1500 in 1545. There is an elaborate monument to them in the church. Much of the material from the priory was used to build a mansion, Ladye Place. Before this, the church was much bigger than it is now. The church is well worth exploring and has the usual guide which also covers the Priory remains.

The East Arms, one of Hurley's pubs, was Eisenhower's unofficial headquarters in the Second World War.

1. From the car park turn left on a public footpath. Cross the river by the bridge and turn right past Hurley Lock to the next bridge.

2. Re-cross the river by the bridge and turn left along the tow path to the next bridge.

3. Cross the river yet again and turn right. Follow the tow path to Marlow.

Across the river is Bisham Abbey. It once belonged to the Knights Templar. Today it is owned by the Sports Council who use it as a national sports centre and a wide variety of sports at a high level are coached here.

The present building is mainly Tudor and was built by Henry VIII for his fourth wife, Anne of Cleeves. For many years it belonged to the Hoby family and they were custodians of Elizabeth I for three years while Mary was on the throne. The building is said to be haunted by the ghost of one Lady Hoby. She punished her little boy for untidiness in his copy book by locking him in a cupboard. Later that day she was called away to another part of the country and it was some time before she returned home. She had forgotten to release her son or tell any one where he was and he had starved to death in the cupboard. She is supposed to roam the building wailing and wringing her hands in remorse. It is said that some blotted sixteenth century copybooks were discovered during renovation work.....

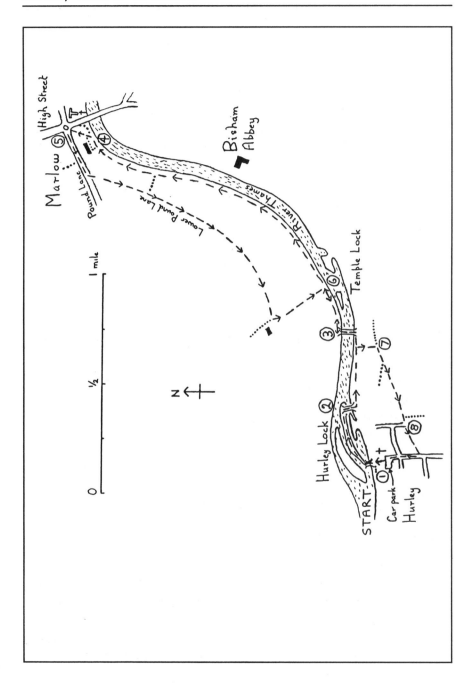

4. As you come into Marlow the tow path is in a park. This is Higginson Park, given to the people of Marlow. Continue through the park to emerge at the bottom of the High Street. The tea shop is just across the road.

Marlow is an ancient and prosperous town with many attractive, mainly Georgian buildings and a remarkable amount of literary association for such a small place. It was already important at the time of the Domesday book and in the thirteenth century returned two members of Parliament.

The most famous structure in Marlow is probably the suspension bridge built by W. Tierney Clarke who also designed the beautiful bridge that connected Buda and Pest across the Danube. The church opposite the entrance to the park is quite modern having been built in 1835. There has been a church on the site since at least 1070. The foundations of the church built in the twelfth century were found to be rotten due to constant damp and flooding and the church was pulled down in 1802. Much that we would find of interest today was destroyed but it has several interesting features covered in the usual guide book.

To explore Marlow, from the tea shop turn right into Station Road and then right down St. Peter Street. This attractive road contains some of the oldest buildings in Marlow. This road led to the original wooden bridge which was replaced by the suspension bridge. It used to be called Duck Lane because the ducking stool was at the end of it. On the river at this point and on the opposite side there used to be very busy wharves: Marlow was an important port sending Chiltern timber, lace and other products to London. Giving the street its name is the Catholic St. Peters church. This contains a relic which is supposed to be the mummified hand of St. James the Apostle. In the pub by the river, the Two Brewers, Jerome K. Jerome wrote some of Three Men in a Boat.

Return to the High Street. The fine building at the top of St. Peter's Street is Marlow Place built in 1721. It was occupied by George II when Prince of Wales and later by his son Prince Frederick. It is presently used as offices.

Many of the buildings on the High Street are Georgian behind their modern shop fronts. The building looking down the High Street which is now the Crown was once the Town Hall. The obelisk outside was erected by the Reading and Hatfield Turnpike Trust. One purpose of this was to shorten the bumping, agonizing journey of the Cecils, martyrs to gout, from Hatfield to the Bath road at Reading. It became known as the Gout Track. The road to the right at the top of the High Street is Spittal Street. Its name comes from the Hospital of St. Thomas run by the Knights of St. John for needy wayfarers in the twelfth century but no trace remains today.

The bridge at Marlow

The road to the left is West Street and it is this which has attracted the literati. Shelley lived at number 104. After his first wife drowned herself he married his mistress Mary and it was while living in Marlow she wrote Frankenstein. Shelley was introduced to Marlow by another poet, Thomas Love Peacock who also lived in West Street at number 47. In more modern times a most prolific writer, G.P.R James lived further along West Street. He is almost entirely forgotten today but in the middle of the nineteenth century was very popular and well known and friends with all the great literary figures of the age. Towards the end of the first World War T.S. Eliot moved to Marlow with his wife to escape the bombing and they lived at number 31 West Street. He travelled to London every day by cycling to Maidenhead to catch the train.

Marlow's most famous son today is a sporting giant. Steve Redgrave has won four Olympic gold medals for rowing and started his career at Great Marlow School.

There is a path to Pound Lane next to the car park in West Street.

5. From the park entrance turn left to walk back in the same direction along Pound Lane. Turn left down a track called Lower Pound Lane and continue for about a mile to a T-junction by a house. Turn left on a track.

6. Turn right along the tow path by the Thames. Cross Temple Bridge to the other bank and turn right. In 150 yards turn left on an unsigned path.

7. At T-junction turn right on a track. Ignore the path on the right into the caravan site.

8. As the track bends right turn left on a fenced path to continue in the same direction. At the road turn right back to the car park.

7. Hambleden Valley

Route: This route must come close to the perfect walk! It wends its way on well maintained paths through beechwoods visiting four small and picturesque villages – Turville, Skirmett, Frieth and Fingest – at the head of the Hambleden Valley. There is almost no road walking except in the villages and there are many fine views of classic Chilterns scenery. This is a walk to take slowly and savour!

Tea shop: The Yew Tree in Frieth is perfectly positioned two thirds of the way round the walk. It started life as the village pub but now is better known for its food. It serves full afternoon teas which include scones with jam and cream, fruit cake and chocolate cake on Saturday and Sunday and any other day when a member of staff is around – ring first to make sure. There is a very pleasant garden at the front. If it seems shut, investigate in the restaurant round the back and tea will be forthcoming.
Tel: 0494 882330

Distance: 6 miles.

Map: Landranger OS 175 Reading and Windsor.

How to get there: The walk starts in the village of Fingest which is hidden in a maze of lanes. Directions are given from the larger village of Lane End which is on the B482 between Marlow and Stokenchurch. From Lane End drive along the B482 towards Stokenchurch for about $^1/_2$ mile and turn left at the crossroads signed Fingest. Follow the road downhill and at the bottom bear right to Fingest. There is space to park next to the church.

Start: The church in Fingest.
SU 911777

Fingest is a very ancient village dating back to Saxon times or earlier. Its name has undergone several metamorphoses for it was originally known as Tinghyrst and may be mentioned in the Domesday book as Dilehurst. The manor of Fingest once belonged to Edward the Confessor. It was presented to the Abbey at St. Albans by Henry I and later came into the possession of the Bishop of Lincoln. One of the bishops built a palace next to the church and the remains can still be seen in a nearby private garden.

The church at Fingest

The glory of the church is its massive Norman tower which is some 60 feet high and 27 feet square. It has three stories. The top one has the remaining bell of the original peal: the rest are supposed to have been lost in a bet between a previous rector and a colleague. The church is basically Saxon though the interior is much changed by Victorian restorers. No wedding in Fingest is supposed to be lucky unless the bride is lifted over the church gate by the groom. After a wedding the gate is locked to make sure the custom is observed. I suppose a bad back is a small price to pay for a lucky marriage.

1. Return to the lane from Lane End and turn right in front of the church. Just past the Church take a public footpath on the right. At a cross path turn left. Cross the lane to continue in the same direction. From the stile follow the clear path half left across the field to a stile and turn left into Turville.

Turville must be the perfect English village with pub, church and village green (and house prices to match). It is overlooked by an impressive white windmill which was featured in the film Chitty Chitty Bang Bang. This is one of the few left of the many that used to be found across the Chilterns. It is now a private house.

There are a couple of interesting stories connected with Turville. Ellen Sadler was born in 1850 and was the tenth child of a family of twelve who lived in one of the small cottages. She was a normal, healthy child and at a young age was sent to Marlow as a nursemaid. She began to have symptoms of drowsiness and a pain in the head and was eventually sent to Reading Hospital. She stayed there for seventeen weeks and was then sent home in a bed on a cart and proclaimed incurable.

Even under her mother's care her condition deteriorated. On March 29th 1871 she said she could hear bells in her head and then went into convulsions. By the time the doctor arrived she had fallen into a sleep that was to last nine years. During this time she never once moved by herself. Her jaw was clenched but she was fed three times a

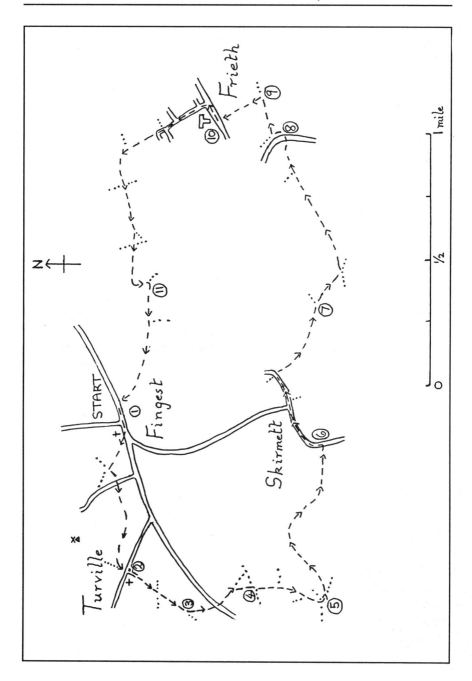

day with port wine and sugar using a small teapot. The liquid passed straight down her throat without any sign of swallowing.

As time went on, people came from far and wide to view the phenomenon. Among them were eminent doctors who, though full of medical terms, could come up with neither a cure nor a definite explanation. They rarely left without a tip for Mother. The local people were sceptical and suspected a fiddle. Nevertheless, it is hard to believe that a young girl would lie in one position without speaking or moving for nine years. And anyway, it must have cost a lot in port wine.

In 1880 her mother died and one of her sisters took over her care. Whether it was due to the fact that her sister stepped up the doses of port wine to every hour and sometimes varied it with tea is not known but Ellen's condition began to improve and she could soon sit up and talk. She could remember nothing of the time while she had been asleep and spoke and acted like the child she had been when she went to sleep though she was now 21. She continued to live in the village and took up bead work for a living. She is said to have married and had twins.

The other story concerns the discovery of a presumed murder. The nave of the little church originally dates from the twelfth century and contained a coffin which was supposed to contain the body of a thirteenth century priest. When it was opened in modern times it was found to contain the skeleton of a woman with bullet marks on one of her bones. She was "in woollen", presumably in accordance with the Act passed at the end of the seventeenth century to aid the wool trade.

2. Take a minor road almost opposite past some cottages. When the road ends continue in the same direction on a public bridleway. This emerges in a field. Ignore the path on the right going uphill and continue in the same direction across the field.

3. After 100 yards fork left and follow the path to a lane. Cross the lane and take the path directly opposite. This goes through a strip of woodland to a field. Do NOT take the obvious path ahead but bear right to the top right-hand corner of the field: this path can be very faint and is often not visible on the ground. Follow the path, marked by a white arrow on a tree, into the wood.

4. After 20 yards turn right on a track and then immediately left on a track going up hill. Continue on this for about $1/2$ mile, ignoring a track on the left part way up the hill.

5. At the top follow the main track round to the left and in 50 yards bear left by a wire fence. Follow the path marked by occasional white arrows on trees through the wood to its edge and then downhill between a wire fence and the wood to a road.

6. Turn left. Go round a sharp right-hand bend and then, as the main road takes a sharp left-hand bend, continue in the same direction on a minor road signed Frieth and Lane End passing the appropriately named Crooked Chimney Cottage. When this road bends left by the Skirmett village sign, turn right on a public bridleway. This path has excellent views over the Hambleden valley on the right.

7. As the path enters a wood ignore the first path on the left. After a $1/4$ mile the path joins a track. Turn immediately left, initially slightly downhill. Follow this through the wood, ignoring the path on the left, and then across a field.

8. Cross the lane and turn left over a stile to follow a path parallel with the road to the far side of the field. Do not cross the stiles ahead and left but turn right to walk down the left-hand side of the field.

9. Half way down the field cross a stile on the left and then immediately cross a second stile to follow a fenced path. At the road turn right to the Yew Tree.

Frieth is a more modern and workaday village than the others visited on this walk but is none the less very attractive. The church was built in 1848 as a chapel of ease to the parish church at Hambleden which was too far away for the growing village. The village was the home of the firm of Collins and West who were famous for their church furniture which they exported around the world.

10. Continue in the same direction for 100 yards then turn left along Ellery Rise. Continue on this road as it changes its name in quick succession to Perrin Springs Road and Spurgrove Lane. When it bends sharply left continue in the same direction along a track and then along a public footpath. Follow this through the woods for $1/2$ mile, ignoring all crossing paths and side turnings, to emerge at a crossing track.

11. Turn right and follow the track to a metal gate. Continue in the same direction across the field to a wood and then stay on the same path downhill through the wood. Just after leaving the wood there is a seat overlooking, in the authors view, the best view in the Chilterns. Carry on downhill at the left-hand side of a field to a stile by a metal gate and then along the left-hand side of another field to the road. Turn left into Fingest.

8. Chisbridge Cross and Booker

Route: This walk goes from Chisbridge Cross through Moor Wood and round Wycombe Air Park to Booker and returns via Beacon Lane. Some of the paths are little used and can be overgrown in summer: not a walk for shorts!

Tea shop: The tea shop is at Booker Garden Centre and is housed in a charming brick and flint cottage. It is open every day from 10am to 5pm during the week and 5.30pm at weekend. Inside there are smoking and no-smoking rooms and, outside, several tables with a view over the centre's display of statuary. It serves sinfully tempting gateaux as well as other cakes, scones and toasted tea-cakes.
Tel: 0494 533945

Distance: 5 miles.

Map: Landranger OS 175 Reading and Windsor.

How to get there: From Marlow High Street turn left along the Henley Road A4155. Take the first right, Oxford Road signed Bovingdon Green, for $2^1/_2$ miles to the entrance to Finnamore Wood.

Start: 50 yards after the entrance to Finnamore Wood is a lane on the left. There is space to pull off the road here.
SU 816890

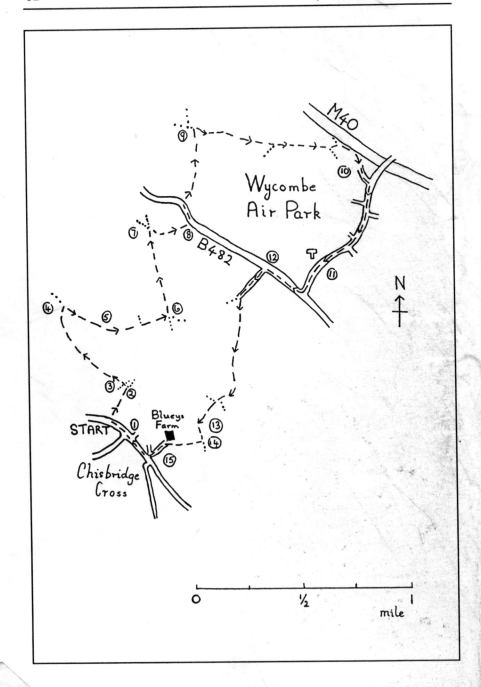

1. Return to the road junction and turn left towards Frieth. After 100 yards take a rising public footpath on the right. This is on a raised bank.

2. The path takes a sharp bend to the right where the bank stops. DO NOT GO THIS WAY. Five yards BEFORE the bank ends take an overgrown path on the left heading towards a white arrow on a tree and a white topped post.

3. Cross a track and take another track ahead also marked by white topped posts. At the time of writing there have been some recent thinning and replanting operations in the wood and so there are many "temporary" tracks made by machinery. Ignore all these and concentrate on following the path marked by the white posts.

4. Near the edge of the wood turn right at a T-junction to almost double back along a track again marked with white topped posts.

5. Continue across a field, where the path is not visible on the ground, to re-enter the wood and again follow the path marked by the familiar white topped posts. Ignore the path on the left marked by a post with a yellow top.

6. At a cross paths at the base of a steep hill turn left.

7. In about 700 yards take a stile on the right. This is not very obvious as it can be overgrown. It is where the path ahead splits in two and opposite a clearing on the left. The path can be very overgrown to start with but soon improves as it goes over a stile and across a field.

8. At the road turn left. Just before a left-hand bend at the bottom of the hill take a signed public footpath on the right into Long Shaw Wood and follow the narrow but clear path through the wood.

9. As the field on the left ends turn sharp right at a T-junction. The path joins a surfaced track round the edge of the air field. **Do not be put off by the notice: the position of the path has been checked with the Rights of Way department at Buckinghamshire County Council.** When the perimeter track bends right, follow the hedge left to a gap onto a path. Turn right and follow the path for a few noisy yards between the hedge and the motorway fence.

Wycombe Air park has been in existence since 1938 and was operated by the RAF until 1962. It is now owned by Wycombe District Council and operated by a private company. It is a very busy airfield for light planes and the majority of the British Gliding team are based here. There is also a company that provides old planes for films and their collection is housed in a museum open to the public.

10. The path emerges at the dead end of a lane. Follow the lane to the road and turn right to Booker Garden Centre in about 600 yards.

The teashop at Booker Garden Centre

11.On leaving the garden centre turn right. At the T-junction turn right again for 300 yards.

12.Turn left down a surfaced lane called Beacon Lane signed public bridleway. When the surfaced road ends take the public bridleway left. After $1/2$ mile ignore the broad path on the left and the narrow path on the right after a further 40 yards.

13.The path takes a sharp left turn alongside a line of pine trees on the right and is signed public bridleway. Do NOT take the unsigned path straight on.

14.Go through the wooden gate and turn immediately right down a broad grassy path.

15.Turn left and left again along the drive to Blueys Farm. At the road turn right back to the starting point in about 300 yards.

9. Ibstone and Stokenchurch

Route: This walk descends from Ibstone on top of the Chilterns into the Wormsly Valley. It then climbs back to Stokenchurch before returning to Ibstone. Much of the walk is in very attractive beechwoods so it makes an ideal walk for a crisp Autumn day when the colours are breathtaking.

Tea shop: The Kings Arms, an old coaching inn in the centre of Stokenchurch, serves teas.
Tel: 0494 483516

Distance: 6 miles. Though not the longest walk in the book, it is probably the most strenuous.

Map: Landranger OS 175 Reading and Windsor and OS 165 Aylesbury and Leighton Buzzard.

How to get there: Ibstone is 2 miles south of junction 5 on the M40 and is signposted from that junction. There are plenty of safe parking spaces beside the common.

Start: From outside The Fox in Ibstone.
SU 752939

Ibstone straggles along the road on top of a ridge. At first glance it appears to have no church, unusual in a village mentioned in the Domesday book. In fact, the delightful little church with much Norman work stands a mile south of the village. It seems that over the centuries the centre of the village has shifted leaving the church at an inconvenient distance. There is evidence that there were once cottages on the lane leading to the church which have been abandoned, perhaps at the time of the Black Death. Legend has it that at one time an attempt was made to build a new church in a more convenient spot nearer the village. The Devil got to hear of it and took a dislike to planned position. During the course of building he removed the structure so many times the builders finally abandoned the idea. Not surprisingly, the spot is now called Hell Corner.

The Fox is a very old pub. The building is about 320 years old. At the end of the last century it was an ale house and the post office and was owned by the local delivery man. It is said to have something rather unusual – a modern ghost! It is reputedly haunted by the ghost of Ted Clack who was a woodsman from the Wormsley estate who was something of a local character (to put it mildly). He died in 1979 and perhaps now stays where he was happiest. His picture is in the public bar.

Thatched cottage on Wormsley Estate

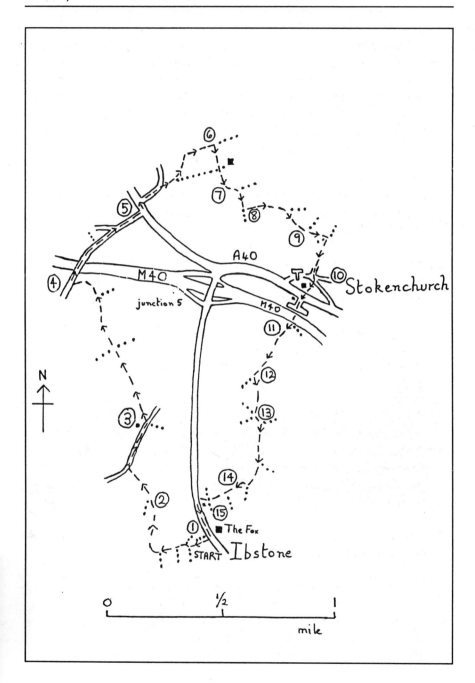

1. With your back to The Fox, turn left along the road for 50 yards and then immediately after a signed public bridleway on the right, turn right on an unsigned path along the right-hand edge of the common. In the corner take the path on the right and follow it round left, ignoring the path on the right on the bend in 20 yards. Follow the path down into the Wormsley valley, ignoring all side paths.

The Wormsley Valley is part of the Wormsley Estate which belongs to the Getty family. It is maintained with no expense spared and much conservation work has been undertaken which has added considerably to the wild life value of the estate.

2. At the bottom of the valley continue in the same direction along the right-hand side of a field. Carry on ahead as the path becomes a track and joins the drive to the mansion.

3. Just past a thatched estate house turn left on a public footpath which rises through woodland. Follow this path for about a mile through the woods ignoring a side turn and a crossing path.

Aston Rowant Nature Reserve is one of several on the scarp slope of the Chilterns. It has areas of chalk grassland with several species of orchids, scrub and mature woodland, predominantly beech. There is a board by the path with further details. Unfortunately, the peace of this lovely spot can be marred by noise from the M40 which cuts through the reserve.

4. The path emerges on a road. Turn right, cross the M40 and continue to a main road, the A40.

A motorway anywhere in the Chilterns is bound to be a disaster but especially so here. The impact of this incursion on the Chiltern skyline would have been lessened if an earlier Ministry of Transport had not ignored all opposition and decided on the present route. An alternative route, put forward by two internationally respected experts Ove Arup and Geoffrey Jellicoe and all the amenity societies, would have cut through woodland to the north-east of the A40 and not ruined what was a beautiful piece of downland and avoided inflicting irreparable damage to Aston Rowant Nature Reserve through which it passes.

5. Turn left and then almost immediately right. As the road bends left take a track on the right to continue in the same direction. After 50 yards take a grassy path half left to pass to the left of a house. Continue on just inside the wood, following the path round to the right.

6. When the field on the right ends, look for a path on the right which is quite easy to miss. It is marked S85 on a post. Walk up the left-hand side of the field, heading to the right of some farm buildings. Cross the stile and a track to a kissing gate and then go straight ahead with a gappy hawthorn hedge on your right.

7. At the end of the field, turn left to go into the wood by way of a stile. After 100 yards, bear right following the white arrows on the trees and keeping just inside the right-hand side of the wood.

8. Just before the end of the wood turn left on path S93 marked with white arrows on trees which again is just inside the wood. After $1/4$ mile the public right of way, marked by white arrows, turns right and descends into a dip and climbs up the other side to join a major path at an elbow.

9. Turn right on this path to continue uphill to a stile by some farm buildings. Turn right then immediately bear left at a junction of tracks. Continue along this track as it becomes a road into Stokenchurch.

Stokenchurch is on one of the highest points of the Chilterns. Its elevation has its drawbacks. In the old days the parish was liable to drought and in the drought of 1870 beer was cheaper than water! The centre is a large village green. The church is tucked away on the north side and is mainly thirteenth century. In the chancel are the brasses of two knights who died in 1410 and 1415 with inscriptions in French.

Just to the north-west of the village is the Post Office Tower, a cylinder of concrete 100m high decorated with radio dishes. It can be seen from Oxford and beyond.

10. At the road by the Royal Oak take the second road on the left. After the last house on the right turn right across the village green to the Kings Arms. Cross the A40 and the village green to the Fleur de Lys pub. Take Coopers Court Road to the left of the pub. Where the road bends left and becomes Slade Road, continue ahead on a public footpath which leads through a tunnel under the M40. At the far end of the tunnel, turn right and then immediately left over a stile into a field.

11. Cross the field diagonally right to a stile in the corner and turn left along the track. The path continues down the right-hand side of the field into a dip and up the other side through a narrow belt of wood and along the right-hand side of a field to a stile.

12. At the stile bear diagonally left across the field to the left of a clump of trees which shelters ponds. After the second pond head for a gate in the right-hand corner of the field.

13. Go left along the track. Where the track bends left, continue in the same direction over a stile and across a field to another stile in the right-hand corner. The path continues in the same direction, eventually entering woodland. At first there is a belt of newly planted trees. After 50 yards bear right into more

mature woodland and follow the path through the woods to a stile into a field.

14. Cross the stile and turn right down the side of the field. At the bottom of the field turn right back into the wood. Ignore an obvious path left but in 50 yards look for a faint path on the left marked by white arrows on the trees. This path is at the point where the trees get larger. Follow the white arrows uphill through the woods.

15. At the top cross a track and continue through a small gate into a garden. Go diagonally to the drive and then up the drive to the lane. Turn left to The Fox in 400 yards.

10. Studley Green

Route: This walk explores the attractive woodlands on either side of the A40 between West Wycombe and Stokenchurch.

Tea shop: The Jardinerie Garden Centre at Studley Green has a tea shop with tables outside in summer. It serves a good range of cakes and is open from 9.30am until 4.30pm.
Tel: 0494 485270

Distance: 4 miles.

Map: Landranger OS 175 Reading and Windsor.

How to get there: A40 between West Wycombe and Stokenchurch. Park on a service road near the Dashwood Arms $1^1/_4$ west of West Wycombe.

Start: At the Dashwood Arms.
SU 807943

1. Turn left up Chipps Hill and then turn right on a public bridleway after 50 yards. By a farm bear right on the main track. Follow the track as it bears sharp left, ignoring a path to right. Continue ahead with a hedge on the left.

2. The path enters a wood. Follow it through the wood: it is clearly defined and marked by occasional white arrows on trees. About 600 yards after entering the wood watch for a cross paths marked by white arrows on a beech tree. Take the path right marked S51. This is about 30 yards before a minor road.

3. At the top of the hill branch half left following the path marked by white arrows.

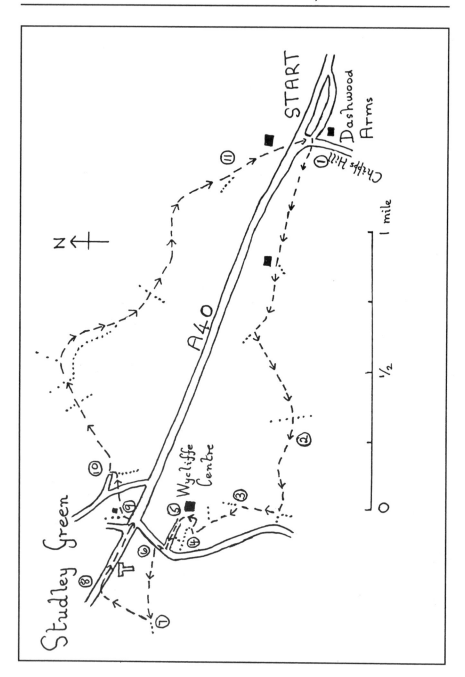

4. The path takes a sharp turn right. After 10 yards bear right between two buildings. DO NOT FOLLOW THE PATH BY THE FENCE LEFT. Continue on the marked path through the Wycliffe Centre, first between hedges and then between a hedge and a building.

   This complex of buildings is the U.K. headquarters of the Wycliffe Bible Translators who exist to translate the Bible into the unwritten languages of the world. They do considerable work in linguistics in association with Reading University and host the summer Institute of Linguistics.

5. At the entrance to the Centre turn left along the drive and then right at a minor road.

6. After 200 yards turn left on a signed public footpath along a drive to houses. At the entrance to The Coppins the path goes between a fence and wall. Cross the stile and go half left across the field to a stile at the far side.

7. In the wood turn right after 30 yards on a path parallel with the edge of the wood.

8. At the A40 turn right to the Jardinerie Garden Centre and the tea shop. From the Jardinerie continue along the A40 in the same direction for 200 yards.

9. 20 yards after St. Francis Road turn left on a signed public footpath down the drive to Nutfield. In front of Nutfield fork right. Continue on this path across a minor road. At the track in front of The Cottage turn left.

10. At a T-junction after 70 yards turn right on a public bridleway and continue on this as it enters Bottom Wood. Follow this path along the valley for about a mile, ignoring all side paths. Leave the wood and continue in the same direction across a field.

Bottom Wood belongs to the Chiltern Society and is used as a demonstration wood. When it was taken over in 1983 it was neglected and in a poor state. It has been transformed into a thriving wood with a mosaic of trees of different ages and a profusion of woodland flowers. From both a wildlife and scenic point of view the improvement has been dramatic. Many groups ranging from primary schools to post graduate students and professional bodies such as the Institute of Chartered Foresters make use of the wood for educational purposes.

11. After passing through a gate the path joins a track. Turn left. The track leads past a farm to the A40 at the Dashwood Arms.

Hanging beech woods

11. Cliveden

Route: This walk is a circuit of the superb gardens and woodlands of the Cliveden estate. This is a National Trust property set high on cliffs in a magnificent setting high above the Thames. The grounds have various gardens and miles of woodland paths. They are open from 11am to 6pm from March to the end of October and from 11am to 4pm in November and December. The house was built in 1851 and is used as a hotel though a couple of rooms are open to the public. Entry is free to National Trust members.

Tea Shop: The tea shop, which also serves morning coffee and light lunches, is in the conservatory. It is not open for teas in November and December.
Tel: 0628 605069

Distance: 3 miles.

Map: Landranger OS 175 Reading and Windsor.

How to get there: The entrance to the estate is on the minor road between Bourne End and Taplow and is well signed.

Start: Car park.
SU 912855

Cliveden Estate has had many owners and the house has been destroyed and rebuilt twice. The first house was built by George Villiers, 2nd Duke of Buckingham, who acquired the estate soon after the Restoration. He also laid out gardens and planted beech woods on what had been barren chalk cliffs above the Thames. The house was burned down in 1795 and remained derelict for several years. It was finally rebuilt in 1824 and then destroyed by fire again in 1849. The present house was built in 1850 – 51. It was the home of the Astor family from 1893 who gave it to the National Trust in 1942. They lived in the house until 1966 and it is now used as a hotel.

The gardens are magnificent and worth visiting many times to admire them at different seasons. I shall briefly mention some of the features but the National Trust book with far more information is for sale at the information kiosk.

However, it must be admitted that Cliveden's fame perhaps rests less on its magnificence than on its connection with one of the famous (infamous?) political scandals of the twentieth century. Cliveden, as the home of Nancy Astor, the first woman to take her seat as an MP, became a centre of political and literary society and this continued after the war. In the late 1950s a friend of the third Viscount called Stephen Ward, an osteopath, rented a small cottage in the grounds. Stephen Ward had some very influential people among his clientele and some people of dubious morals among his friends. To what extent the two categories overlapped is not known.

In 1961 the Viscount and his wife were entertaining the Minister for War, John Profumo, and his wife for the weekend while at the same time Stephen Ward was entertaining a prostitute called Christine Keeler and a Russian diplomat in his cottage. This led to a brief affair between Christine Keeler and John Profumo which he broke off when the Foreign Office found out about it and warned him of its unsuitability. This all came to the public's notice because Christine Keeler was attacked while she was visiting her friend, Mandy Rice-Davies, the mistress of a slum property racketeer called Rachman. The nation was electrified by the revelations at the trial. Profumo lied to the House of Commons which ended his political career and helped to precipitate the fall of Prime Minister Macmillan. Stephen Ward was made the scapegoat and was arrested for living on immoral earnings. When his well placed friends failed to come to his rescue he committed suicide by taking an overdose of sleeping pills.

1. Leave the car park by the information kiosk. Take the path on the left and branch left after 25 yards into the Water Garden.

   This garden was created by Lord Astor in 1893 from an area of parkland containing a stagnant duck pond and the pond was further enlarged in 1905. The pagoda on the island was originally made for the Paris exhibition of 1867. This garden is particularly lovely in spring with primroses and white daffodils under cherry trees.

2. After exploring the Water Garden, retrace your steps and follow the road in front of the car park to the Fountain of Love ahead. There are fine views of the house to the left.

   The fountain was made for the 1st Viscount Astor by Thomas Waldo Story, an American sculptor living in Rome. The women, attended by cupids, are supposed to have discovered the fountain of love and have been carried away by it which accounts for their expressions!

The Fountain of Love

3. On the far side of the fountain go through a gap in the hedge
   on the right into the Long Garden and walk the length of the
   Long Garden.

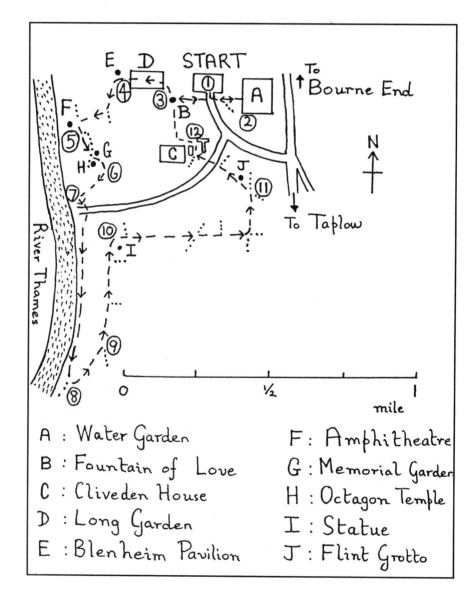

A : Water Garden

B : Fountain of Love

C : Cliveden House

D : Long Garden

E : Blenheim Pavilion

F : Amphitheatre

G : Memorial Garden

H : Octagon Temple

I : Statue

J : Flint Grotto

This too was created at the behest of the 1st Viscount Astor and reflects his love of the Italian Renaissance. There is some fine topiary and on the long south facing wall are several unusual shrubs.

4. At the far end turn right past the Blenheim Pavilion and downhill. After 70 yards turn right downhill on a grass path towards the river and the amphitheatre. Turn left.

The Blenheim Pavilion is a folly was built about 1727 for the then owner of Cliveden, the Earl of Orkney. He was one of the Duke of Marlborough's most trusted generals and commanded a brigade at the Battle of Blenheim which this pavilion is supposed to commemorate. The 1st Viscount Astor commissioned a statue of Marlborough from the designer of the Fountain of Love. It stood in the centre, framed by the arch, until it was damaged by vandals who also caused extensive damage to the building.

The amphitheatre was also built by Lord Orkney. Its main claim to fame is that it was the stage for the first performance of Rule Britannia as part of the masque Alfred written by Arnes for Frederick, Prince of Wales in 1740. Frederick rented Cliveden from 1739 until his death and used it as a country retreat. It was while he was at Cliveden that he was hit in the chest by a cricket ball whilst playing with his children and this led to his death.

5. As the path starts to rise take the branch right along Honeymoon Walk. Continue on past the steps on the left. There is a superb view of the Thames from here. If you look behind and up, there is a large old oak. This is known as Canning's Oak because the statesman is supposed to have spent many hours here admiring the view. At a T-junction turn right. (10 yards to the left is the Memorial Garden). After 50 yards branch left uphill and then go up the steps to the Octagon Temple.

The Memorial Garden was originally conceived as an Italian garden but during the First World War it was made into a cemetery for those who died in the hospital built on the estate. The Octagon Temple was built by Lord Orkney in 1735. When the Astor family bought the estate it was converted into a chapel and several members of the Astor family are buried there. From the Octagon Temple there is a good view of the house and across the most formal part of the gardens, the Parterre.

6. Turn right down a grassy slope to the river.

This is the Yew Tree Walk planted by Lord Orkney. The yews were intended to make a formal clipped hedge but were allowed to grow up when the fashion in landscape design changed to more naturalistic effects.

7. Turn left along the river bank for about $1/2$ mile.

8. After $1/2$ a mile, at a point where the path no longer hugs the river bank, take a path on the left going back the way you have come but uphill.

9. At the top turn left onto a high level path above the river. This is the Grand Walk. Ignore all paths on the right.

10. When the house is in view ahead turn right in front of the statue of the Duke of Sutherland. Continue across one cross track to a second cross track and turn left.

This statue was sculpted in 1866 and originally stood at the end of the Main Avenue where the Fountain of Love is now. It was moved to its present position 1895.

11. At a smaller crossing path turn left downhill to pass the Flint Grotto on the right. Follow the path into the valley and up the other side ignoring a path on the right and crossing a surfaced drive. At a T-junction turn right up some steps. At the top, by the side of the house, turn right to the tea shop in the Orangery. There is a good view from the terrace if you turn left.

12. Leaving the tea room, turn left and then left to the front of the house. Turn right up the main drive to the Fountain of Love and retrace your steps to the car park.

12. West Wycombe and Bradenham

Route: This walk connects two villages, both attractive though very different and both in the care of the National Trust. The outward route has an exhilarating ridge walk and the return is through some beautiful beech-woods. This is a short but strenuous walk. Allow plenty of time for it because there are so many inter-esting things to see at West Wycombe and such won-derful views to enjoy.

Tea shop: The biggest problem on this walk is going to be to decide where to have tea. West Wycombe Garden Centre has a tea shop with a very pleasant garden with a view of the Chilterns and excellent home-made cakes. Alternatively, the Bread Oven Tea Rooms, behind the Village Store in the High Street, is a tradi-tional tea shop. The building was a bakery until the early 1950s and the ovens have been restored and form the focal point of the tea shop. A range of speciality teas is on offer as well as the usual temp-tations. In addition, teas are served in the Parish Rooms half-way along the High Street on Sunday in summer.
Tel: 0494 438635 (West Wycombe Garden Centre)
0494 526439 (West Wycombe Village Store)

Distance: 4 miles.

Map: Landranger OS 175 Reading and Windsor and OS 165 Aylesbury and Leighton Buzzard.

How to get there: From the A4010 High Wycombe – Aylesbury road take the road signed Bradenham. There is a small parking space on the left next to the Youth Hostel.

Start: From the church in Bradenham.
SU 828972

*Bradenham Manor House, next to the church, was rented by Isaac
Disraeli from 1829 until his death in 1848 and his son, Benjamin,
spent much of his youth here. Benjamin was intended for a career in
the law but took to literature and politics instead, producing several
novels before entering Parliament. In "Endymion" the village of
Hurstley is Bradenham. He loved the Chilterns all his life. and finally
made his home at Hughenden, just over the hills. He was buried there
in preference to Westminster Abbey.*

*Isaac Disraeli was a distinguished man in his own right and an
authority on antiquarian books. Jewish by ancestry, Isaac Disraeli
became a member of the Anglican church along with his children and
the church next to the Manor House, St. Botolph's, has a memorial to
him.*

*The church is originally Saxon but of course has alterations and
additions from every age. It boasts two of the oldest bells in England
dating from 1250 and has the usual informative booklet within.
Another distinction of Bradenham is that it is one of the very few
places to remain in possession of its Saxon owners after the Norman
Conquest though they did acquire a Norman overlord.*

1. After visiting the church walk back to the A4010 at The Red
   Lion. Turn right for 50 yards and then take a public footpath
   on the left through a metal kissing gate.

2. Follow the path diagonally right over the railway line and on
   up the hill, ignoring branches on the right, into a wood where
   the path is clearly marked.

3. At the top of the hill, at Nobles Farm, turn left on a crossing
   track which soon becomes a path. Follow this path along the
   ridge, enjoying the excellent views, for about $1^1/_4$ miles to the
   National Trust car park on top of West Wycombe Hill.

4. Leave the path and walk across to the building with the golden
   ball on top. This is St. Lawrence's Church. Take the path by the
   side of the church to the Mausoleum. From the Mausoleum

follow the obvious path downhill towards High Wycombe, spread out at your feet. After 100 yards turn right down some steps and continue across the hill side in the same direction when the steps end. West Wycombe Garden Centre with its tea shop is across the road.

West Wycombe from West Wycombe Hill

St Lawrence's church is built in the ditch and bank of an Iron Age hill fort and is an ancient foundation. It was originally the parish church of the "lost" village of Haveringdon. This was once a little way along the ridge and was abandoned in the late eighteenth century, probably due to lack of water. Only the ruined chancel and part of the tower remained when Sir Francis Dashwood turned his attention to it. He rebuilt the church in his beloved classical style and the nave is like a Georgian drawing room with stalls and lectern that

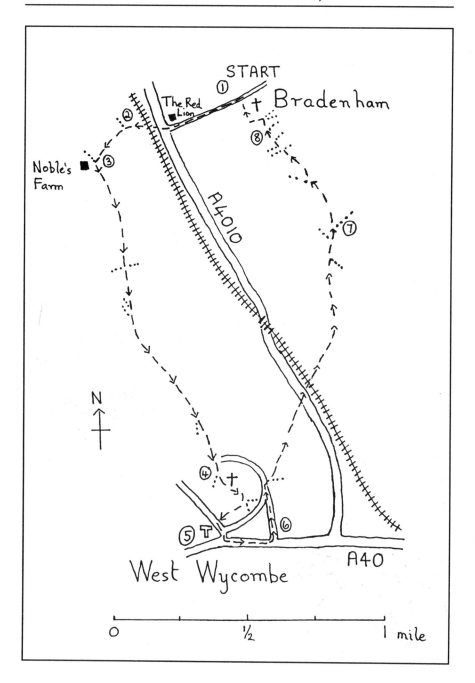

are comfortable rosewood armchairs, exquisite paintings and stucco decorations on the ceiling and walls and a marble floor. Some brasses and monuments from the original church were preserved.

The most unusual feature of all is the golden ball on top of the tower. It holds ten or twelve people and is reached by a ladder on the outside. John Wilkes, a friend of Dashwood's, described it as "the best Globe tavern I was ever in".

The fortifications which defended the iron age village can be seen running parallel with the churchyard fence and at the eastern end are cut by the mausoleum. This is a large open hexagon of flint with Portland stone dressing. It contains memorials to members of the Dashwood family and their friends. For example, in the centre is an urn on a pedestal commemorating Francis Dashwood's wife who died in 1769.

5. From the Garden Centre walk down the road towards the village and turn left along the High Street. The Bread Oven Tea Room is on the left.

For more than 250 years West Wycombe has been associated with the Dashwood family. West Wycombe village was purchased from Sir John Dashwood in 1929 and given to the National Trust five years later so that it could be preserved as a living example of an English village. Only two new houses have been built in this century. The village has examples of many types of English architecture from the sixteenth century on and is well worth taking the time to explore in detail. The National Trust produce an "architectural trail guide" round the village which can be bought from the village shop opposite the George and Dragon.

The present West Wycombe House and Park was given to the National Trust by the present Sir Francis Dashwood in 1943. The house was rebuilt in the late 1700s by a previous Sir Francis, now best remembered for the Hellfire Club, of which more later. He was a much travelled and cultivated man who was interested in classical architecture. *He had the house rebuilt in the Palladian style, dammed the infant River Wye to form a lake and employed Humphrey Repton to lay out the grounds. The house is open to the public in June, July and August, Sunday to Thursday from 2 until 6. The grounds only are also open in April and May on Wednesday and Sunday from 2 till 6.*

6. Turn left up Church Lane under the clock. (To visit the famous Hellfire Caves bear left near the top of the hill.) 40 yards after a road joins on the left go through a wooden kissing gate on the right and then bear half left across the field. Cross the main road and follow the same path over the railway lines and on through a wood uphill. Near the top the wood thins out to give extensive views and joins a larger path to continue in the same direction. Continue on the path marked by white arrows as far as a fork marked by white arrows on a tree. Ignore all unmarked side paths.

Sir Francis Dashwood, the 2nd Baronet, succeeded to his father's estate and fortune when he was sixteen. He was a man of considerable energy, wealth and achievement, not to say profligacy. He was Chancellor of the Exchequer (said to be the worst ever at the time) and Postmaster General. He rewrote the Book of Common Prayer into every day English and built the straight road into High Wycombe you can see from the top of the hill.

Today his popular reputation is solely concerned with the Hellfire Club, supposedly founded for the practice of black magic, first at Medenham Abbey and then in these caves. The name the group gave themselves was the Brotherhood of St. Francis or Dashwood's Apostles and half of Dashwood's Cabinet colleagues were members. They were undoubtedly up to no good but wild parties are more likely than devil worship.

The caves are not natural. They were dug to provide raw materials for the new road to High Wycombe that Dashwood built to relieve local poverty and unemployment. They go back into the hill side for about quarter of a mile and are cleaned out and lit and provided with displays supposed to recreate times past.

7. 120 yards after the fork turn right on a narrow, unmarked path. This is very easy to miss. Though the start of this path is unmarked it is soon indicated again by the usual white arrows. This is the edge of Naphill Common which is notorious for being a maze of unmarked and unmapped paths so watch for the white arrows and follow the path they show to a track.

8. Turn left to Bradenham. Leave the track and walk in front of the manor house and church back to the start.

13. Beaconsfield
Old Town

Route: This walk explores part of the southern edge of the Chilterns and has the virtue of being unusually flat for the Chilterns having only two very short climbs.

Tea shop: The Old Tea House in Beaconsfield Old Town is in a pleasant position opposite the church. It offers the usual array of goodies including scones with real clotted cream. It is open 9am – 5pm Tuesday to Saturday and 1.30pm – 5.30pm on Sunday. There are tables outside in summer.
Tel: 0494 676273

Distance: 6 miles.

Map: Landranger OS 175 Reading and Windsor.

How to get there: Follow the signs to Hedgerley Green from the A355, Slough to Beaconsfield road.

Start: The walk starts from Hedgerley. There is a narrow layby just north of the White Horse. This is where the walk finishes. If this is full, there are other parking spots elsewhere in the village.
SU 969875

Hedgerley is a picture postcard village which takes great pride in itself. It has won the best kept village competition several times. This does not concern itself with how pretty a village is but how well it is cared for. Hedgerley, having an attractive combination of buildings and residents who care for it, is a real gem. It was formerly a centre for brick making as witnessed by the name of one of the pubs and there are traces of clay pits round the village. The church is quite modern having been built in 1852 to replace an earlier one which was demolished. It contains a number of objects from the previous church including a piece of seventeenth century velvet which comes from a cloak given by Charles II as an altar cloth.

Hedgerley village pond

1. Walk past the White Horse and through Hedgerley. Turn right by the Brickmould up Kiln Lane and carry on along this lane for 600 yards to a T-junction. Cross Andrew Hill Lane and continue ahead on a public bridleway through a gate opposite.

2. After 300 yards turn right on a track immediately in front of the first farm building. This is marked by a white arrow on a telegraph pole. After a stile the track peters out. Continue on the right-hand side of the field towards the right-hand corner of a wood and another stile.

3. The path now bears left along Dorney Bottom and stays close to the wood on the left to the A355.

4. Turn right along the road for 250 yards and then take a public footpath over a stile on the left. The path continues along Dorney Bottom. It is not always clear on the ground but stays close to the wood on the right.

5. Cross the stile onto a minor road and turn right.

6. 40 yards after the drive to Woodlands Farm look for a stile on the right. The path rises steeply and can be overgrown. Near the top it emerges onto a much clearer path. Turn left to a stile and follow the path ahead to a kissing gate onto a minor road.

7. Turn right for 40 yards to a stile on the left. Follow the clear path as it goes through fields and small woods to a stile onto a minor road.

8. Turn left for 20 yards then right to meet a surfaced path in 10 yards. Turn left. The path turns sharp right over a footbridge over the M40.

9. At the far side of the footbridge take a surfaced path on the left which follows the road into Beaconsfield Old Town. The tea shop is on the right, opposite the church.

When the railway came to Beaconsfield, the station was built a mile away. Beaconsfield New Town has grown up round the station and the Old Town has kept its separate personality. It grew up at the

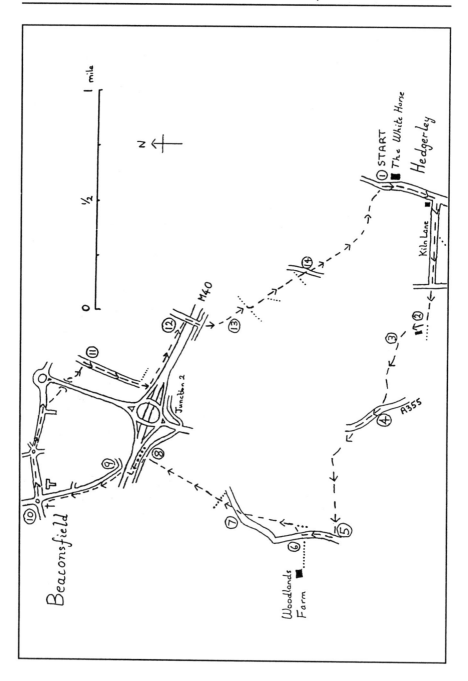

*crossroads of the coach roads to Windsor and Oxford and the roads,
called Ends, were packed with inns. To get to this haven the coaches
had to travel through wild, wooded country in constant danger from
highwaymen. The local saying was "Here, if you beat a bush, 'tis
odds you'll start a thief." One of the most notorious highwaymen of
his day, Jack Shrimpton, was born at Penn, a few miles away, and
operated round here.*

*Several colourful and important people have lived in Beaconsfield.
Probably the most influential was Edmund Burke, the eighteenth
century political thinker. He was the son of an Irish Protestant father
and Catholic mother and taught by the Quakers. His thinking was
characterised by opposition to oppression and he campaigned against
slavery and the exploitation of India. Disraeli thought so highly of
him that when he was made a peer he took the name Earl of
Beaconsfield in his honour. G. K. Chesterton wrote the Father Brown
stories for which he is famous while living in Beaconsfield. Enid
Blyton was another resident; perhaps Noddy and Bigears really lived
at Bekonscot, the model village nearby.*

10. At the roundabout turn right and continue straight on across
    another roundabout. 100 yards after Burnham Avenue take a
    public footpath on the right. This is the old A40. At the far side
    of the tunnel under the new road the path bears right into a
    narrow strip of woodland.

11. Cross the stile onto a minor road and turn right. Follow the
    road until it ends and then continue ahead in the same direc-
    tion on a path. When the path appears to end turn sharp left on
    a path parallel with the M40. This ends at some steps up onto a
    farm drive.

12. Turn right and over the M40. Cross the road to a public
    footpath opposite. Follow the path along the right-hand side of
    a field and then bear left past an isolated tree to a wood.

13. Enter the wood. The path shortly reaches a farm road. Turn right and then left after 30 yards to continue in the wood. At the top of a short climb, when the main track bears right, continue ahead on a clear path.

14. At a lane turn right then left over a stile after 50 yards. Go half right across the field and follow a clear path across three more fields back to the starting point.

14. Seer Green and Chalfont St. Giles

Route: This walk is along footpaths linking two prosperous and attractive Chiltern villages. Hodgemoor Wood, on the first part of the route, is exceptionally attractive and there are some fine views.

Tea shop: The tea shop on this walk, Tea Time, is in the centre of Chalfont St. Giles. It is a traditional tea shop open from 9.30am to 5.30pm Monday to Saturday and 2.30pm to 5.30pm on Sunday throughout the year. It sells a good range of cakes and has some tables outside at the front in the summer.
Tel: 0494 871099

Distance: 5 miles.

Map: Landranger OS 175 Reading and Windsor.

How to get there: From the A355 Beaconsfield – Amersham road 1 mile north of the A40 take a minor road signed Seer Green. After about a mile turn left on a road again signed Seer Green. Park in the centre of the village near the church.

Start: From Holy Trinity Church in Seer Green.
SU 965919

Seer Green was mentioned in the Domesday Book as La Sere but was a hamlet until the coming of the railway made it a convenient place for commuters to London to live.

1. Take the road past the Three Horseshoes and the shops (Orchard Road). Next to number 27 is an unsigned footpath. Follow this between houses across two roads to emerge in a field.

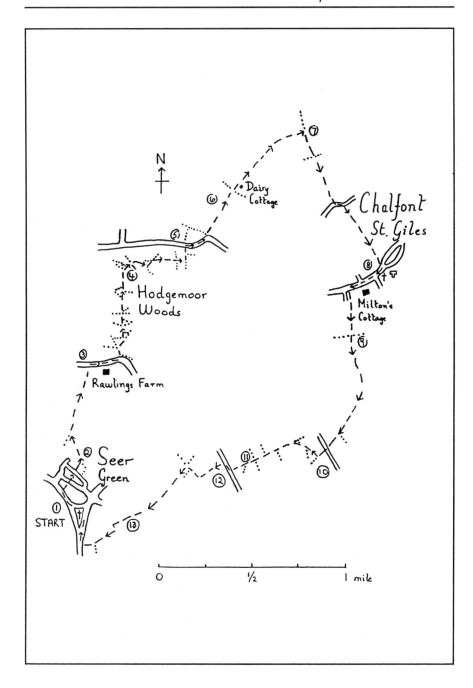

2. Bear diagonally left to a stile and turn right on a fenced path. Cross the stile and continue ahead on the right-hand side of two fields with a wood on the right. Go over another stile and continue ahead, with a fence and field on the right, to a lane.

3. Turn right. After $1/4$ mile, past Rawlings Farm, the road bends sharply right and there are several signed footpaths and horse trails into Hodgemoor wood on the left. Turn left into the wood and after 15 yards fork right onto a path signed horse trail. After a further 20 yards branch left on a path with a no horses sign. Follow this path for $1/2$ mile ignoring all cross paths and side turns: some are horse trails and some are concerned with forestry operations.

4. At a complex junction, where the left branch is marked by a red topped post, turn right. After 70 yards, the main path bears right. Continue in the same direction on a smaller path for about 300 yards to a T-junction with a cross path. Turn left and at a cross path after 75 yards, turn right. Follow this path, crossing another path to another T-junction. Turn left to a lane.

(Note: it is easy to miss the path in Hodgemore Wood as it is a maze of unmarked paths. If this happens, head north to come out on a lane and turn right to pick up the route at point 5.)

5. Turn right and walk round a left-hand bend. At a right-hand bend take a track on the left and then immediately turn right on a signed public footpath through a small gate on the right. Walk along the left-hand side of the field. The views to the right extend as far as London on a clear day.

6. At the far end of the field go over a stile and follow a broad path between fences. At a T-junction turn right and then left on a track in 20 yards. After Dairy Cottage this becomes a path between hedges. Cross the stile and continue down the left-hand side of the field. Cross another stile. In this field the path is not visible on the ground. Go ahead and slightly right to a stile in the fence at the far side.

7. After 20 yards at a T-junction turn right and follow the path to a road. Turn left for 60 yards then right on a track marked footpath and South Bucks Way. When the track ends continue ahead on the path. Follow this and it eventually becomes a track again leading to Chalfont St Giles. When it emerges in the middle of the village, the tea shop is across the road, slightly left.

Chalfont St. Giles, like all the villages in this part of the Chilterns, has seen considerable modern expansion with the growth of commuting. However, the centre of Chalfont St. Giles is still very picturesque with its village green surrounded by old cottages, shops and pubs. The church is of twelfth century origin and has some famous medieval wall paintings. The graveyard has an unusually wide variety of headstones and memorials, many bearing epitaphs. One was obviously written by someone who felt he had travelled far enough:

Italy and Spain, Germany and France,
Have been on earth my weary Dance.
So that I own the grave's my dearest Friend
That to my travels it has put an End.

The church is reached through a gate by the tea shop.

The most famous building in Chalfont St. Giles is Milton's cottage. From the name and because it is a museum full of Milton memorabilia you might imagine that the poet spent all his life here. In fact, he lived in the house for nine months in the plague year of 1665. The house was found for him by his pupil and friend, Thomas Ellwood and while living here he finished Paradise Lost and started Paradise Regained. The museum has first editions of both as well as other exhibits and a beautifully maintained and charming cottage garden. The cottage is the only house still in existence where Milton is known to have lived. It was bought by public subscription in 1887 to commemorate Queen Victoria's Jubilee with the Queen herself heading the subscription list with £20. It is open Tuesday to Saturday, 10am to 1pm and 2pm to 5pm and on Sunday from 2pm to 5pm from March to October.

Chiltern scenery, near Chalfont St. Giles

8. From the tea shop turn left and walk up the road for 300 yards to Milton's Cottage. Carry on up the road for another 100 yards and just before Hillside Close take a signed footpath on the left. Follow this uphill, ignoring a footpath on the left, to emerge on a playing field. Carry on along the left-hand side and at the far end continue ahead with the Bowling Club hut on the right. Beyond the bowling green carry on along the left-hand side of the field to a gate onto a track.

9. Continue on a signed footpath immediately opposite. The path is narrow and can be overgrown in summer. Do not take the clear branch on the left but continue by the fence to a road.

10. Cross the road and take the path directly opposite over a very substantial stile. At a fork in 100 yards bear right. As the path leaves the wood fork left and follow it along the left-hand side of three fields.

11.Immediately after passing under some pylons navigate an awkward wooden barrier and continue ahead, now on the right-hand side of four small fields and along a broad tree lined path to a road.

12.Turn right for 125 yards and then left up a track signed public footpath. As the track bends left to a house, cross the stile ahead and turn right on a clear path. In the corner of the field cross a stile and after 25 yards turn left on a clear path across a field and then along the left-hand side of a playing field.

13.In the corner of the playing field the path bears left to go round the edge of Seer Green with houses on the right. Ignore branches on the right into the houses and continue until the path ends at a broad track. Turn right between brick walls and at the road turn right again to the church.

15. Little Missenden and Amersham Old Town

Route: The walk starts in the very pretty village of Little Missenden. It climbs through some very attractive scenery with excellent views, especially in winter when the leaves are off the trees, before dropping down to Amersham. There is a little road walking to get out of Amersham but the return to Little Missenden up the Misbourne valley, past Shardloes Lake, is well worth it.

Tea shop: The Tea and Coffee Shop is on the High Street in Amersham Old Town. It is in a very old building with a few tables in a small, flowery courtyard at the back. It offers a wide variety of cakes and cream teas with clotted cream. The shop also sells an impressive range of teas and coffees.
Tel: 0494 432126

Distance: 5 miles.

Map: Landranger OS 165 Aylesbury and Leighton Buzzard.

How to get there: Turn off the A413 Amersham – Aylesbury road on a minor road through Little Missenden. Park on the road side near the Crown which is at the east end of the village near the A413.

Start: At the Crown.
SU 927988

Little Missenden, having been neglected by the advance of the railway escaped the advance of Metroland which had such a profound influence on much of this part of the Chilterns. It is everyone's idea of what an English village should be with ancient church, Manor House and old coaching inns grouped together to charming effect. The

*church, near the centre of the village, is of no great architectural
merit, perhaps, but is worth exploring because if its great age. It is
said that the most recent addition is the porch added in 1450. It was
founded by the Saxons but has some Roman bricks in the chancel
arch. Perhaps the most interesting features are the wall paintings.
These brightly coloured pictures were usual in medieval churches
where the congregation was mostly illiterate. Later, in Puritan times,
they fell from fashion and were painted over and the majority have
been lost. A few, like these, remain to give us a glimpse into the past.*

*One resident of Little Missenden was Dr. Bates who lived in the
Manor House by the church. He was doctor to Francis Dashwood of
West Wycombe and the longest survivor of the Hell Fire Club (see
walk 12, page 79). It certainly didn't do him any harm as he lived to
be ninety-eight. To the end of his life he maintained that the stories
were fabrications and political smears.*

1. Almost opposite the Crown take an unsurfaced track past
   Tobys Lane Farm. When the track bends left continue in the
   same direction on a path. This is a very old, sunken path with
   excellent views glimpsed through the hedge as you climb. 50
   yards after a wood starts on the right, fork left to continue
   along the left-hand side of the wood.

2. When the wood on the right ends continue with a field on the
   right for about 250 yards. The path bends right and at this
   point there is a stile on the left.

3. The path is not usually apparent on the ground. It goes
   diagonally right to a hedge gap (though it may be easier to
   walk round the edge of the field). It then continues in the same
   direction across the next field and along the left-hand side of
   the one after that. Across the next field the path bears slightly
   left to a stile and does not follow the obvious path leading to
   Mop End Farm buildings.

4. Over the stile continue along the lane in the same direction for
   100 yards and then turn left on a signed public footpath.
   Follow this path through woods and fields, gently downhill,
   for $1^1/_2$ miles. Ignore any side turns which are all concerned

with woodland management or the sub station passed on the right. After about a mile the path becomes somewhat less distinct on the ground but continues with a field on the left and a line of trees on the right towards a cream house. The path ends at the drive to Shardeloes House at Lower Park House.

5. Turn right for 10 yards then right again on a public footpath through a metal kissing gate. Follow the path half left into a dip and up the other side. Continue on across a surfaced track to a stile onto the main road, the A413.

6. 25 yards to the right the path carries on over a stile and down some steps. Follow this path through a small plantation and along the left-hand side of the field to a lane. Cross the lane and continue in the same direction. The path ends by the entrance to the grave yard.

7. After 10 yards turn left through the grounds of the Baptist Chapel to the High Street. The tea shop is to the right, past the Market House.

Amersham is the northern extremity of the Metropolitan Line but fortunately the railway stopped on common land above the old town and so modern Amersham-on-the-Hill developed separately from Old Amersham which thus remained intact and has a fine diversity of buildings from the fifteenth century onwards. It is well worth spending some time exploring.

Amersham is recorded in the Domesday book as Agmodesham and has also been called Elmodesham, Amundesham and Homersham! It has a charter granted by King John in 1200 granting permission to hold a market and a fair every September. The building in the road is the Market Hall built by Sir William Drake in 1682 and market stalls are still erected among its arches. In the corner was a lock up for the drunks and rogues.

There are many old coaching inns along the High Street since Amersham was once an important stop on the route from London to

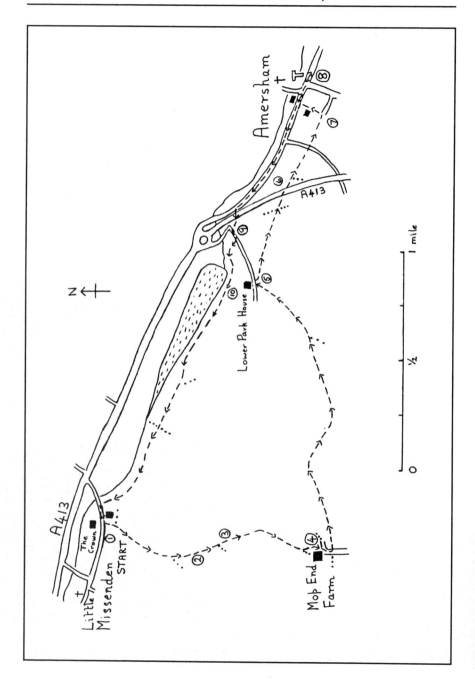

Aylesbury and points North. The Crown looks quite modern because it has suffered two disastrous fires in its 300 year history. The magistrates court used to be held in the bar and there was a regular coach service from the Crown to the Old Bell in Holborn until 1890. Cromwell is said to have dined at the Griffin. The most picturesque is perhaps the black and white King's Head.

Amersham used to be famous as a centre of religious dissent, particularly Lollards and later Quakers. In 1506 six people were burned on the hill above the town where the Martyr's Memorial now stands One of the martyrs was William Tylsworth and it is said that his own daughter was forced to light the fire.

The Market Hall, Amersham

8. From the tea shop turn right and walk back along the High Street and out of the town. The path on the left-hand side of the road eventually emerges on the by pass, the A413 again. Cross this and take a small lane by the 300 yard junction warning sign.

9. When this joins the drive to Shardeloes House turn left and after 25 yards turn right on a signed public footpath by the cricket pitch. Follow the track round behind the pavilion and then bear right to a gate where the path to Little Missenden starts.

The large white house on the hill is Shardloes. It was the home of the Drake family. In 1602 Joan Tothill, eldest of the thirty three children of William Tothill of Shardloes, was forced to marry Francis Drake of Esher against her will. From this unhappy union descended the Drake family who dominated Amersham and controlled the rotten borough for over two hundred years. The present house was built by Stiff Leadbetter and Robert Adam between 1758 and 1766. The grounds, including the lake, were laid out by Humphrey Repton. The house has now been divided up into apartments and it is not open to the public.

10. This is a popular and well walked path. It starts with a short fenced section and then goes along the right-hand side of a large field with Shardeloes Lake on the right. Near the end of the field it bears left, slightly uphill, to a double stile and then joins a very clear path which leads to the road in Little Missenden, crossing another track on the way.

16. Princes Risborough

Route: The route follows one of the most beautiful sections of the Ridgeway from Great Kimble over Pulpit Hill and Whiteleaf Hill, with its landmark cross, to Princes Risborough. It returns along the foot of the Chiltern escarpment passing through the attractive villages of Monks Risborough and Askett.

Tea shop: This is behind Well End Antique Centre in Bell Street, Princes Risborough. It does a good selection of home made cakes and the fruit cake is especially recommended. The building is sixteenth century but was seriously damaged by fire in 1989 when a car caught fire outside. It re-opened in 1990. There is a very pleasant garden. The tea shop is open 9.30am to 5.30pm Monday to Saturday and 1.30pm to 5.30pm on Sunday and Bank Holidays.

Tel: 0844 275902

Distance: $5^1/_2$ miles.

Map: Landranger OS 165 Aylesbury and Leighton Buzzard.

How to get there: The walk starts on the A4010 Princes Risborough – Aylesbury road at a layby with a distinctive thatched house. This is 2 miles north of Princes Risborough and $^1/_4$ mile S southf the junction between the A4010 and a minor road signed to Wendover.

Start: At the north end of the layby.

SP 825058

1. Turn up a public bridleway signed North Bucks Way. Ignore a path on the left after $^1/_4$ mile and on the right after a further 100 yards.

2. After another 100 yards take a stile by a wooden gate on the right. Follow the path round to the left and after 50 yards turn right on a cross path. This is the Ridgeway. Go down into a dip and up the other side, ignoring branches on the left until you come to a wooden gate. The path is contouring along the side of Pulpit Hill.

   This is the Ridgeway. For more information see page 4.

   Pulpit Hill was crowned by a large iron age fort. This is supposed to have been the site of Cymbeline's Castle where the British King Cunobelinus fought the Romans in the first century A.D.

3. The Ridgeway turns right here on a crossing path but a much more attractive route is to continue straight across to follow a path downhill. Soon after the path narrows it splits into two: the left-hand branch is the drier footpath, the right is a bridleway which can be very muddy. At the road turn left to The Plough and rejoin the Ridgeway.

   (If you want to stay on the Ridgeway turn right along the track and left after 20 yards. A short path leads into a field. Cross this and enter a wood. The path goes down steeply between wire fences to a road. Turn left to the Plough.)

4. Turn right on a bridleway just beyond the Plough. After 50 yards turn left and go over a stile by a gate into a beech wood. When the path splits take the right-hand branch and follow the Ridgeway steeply uphill to the summit of Whiteleaf Hill. At the top the trees give way and for the best view go to the edge of the escarpment above the cross protected by a wooden rail.

   Cut into the side of Whiteleaf Hill is Whiteleaf Cross. It has a triangular base and arms nearly 7m wide with a span of over 26m.

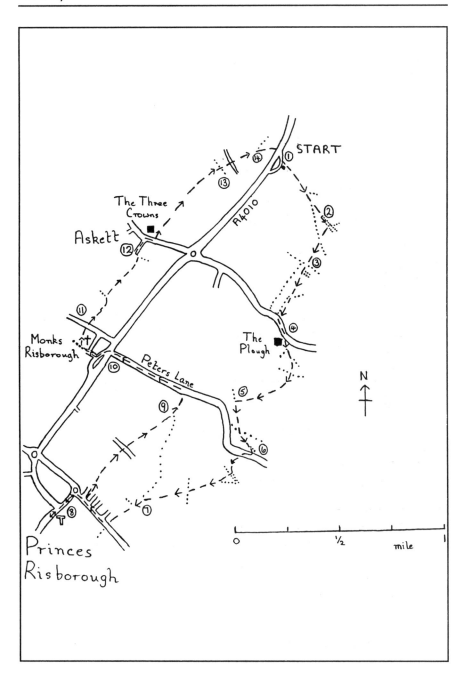

Like the nearby Bledlow Cross, its origins are obscure but as a charter of A.D. 903 refers to a boundary mark here, it is likely to be of ancient origin. It cannot really be seen when you are standing above it but later in the walk it is clear.

The small mound covered in trees is a Neolithic burial chamber. It was excavated in the 1930s. A timber burial chamber was found with the remains of a middle aged man together with flint tools and fragments of pottery.

5. Retrace your steps for a few yards to a cross path with the mound on your right and turn right. Follow this path to a road, ignoring a cross path and a path left to the car park.

6. At the road turn right for 20 yards and then take a track on the left and follow it round to a stile. Over the stile do not take the obvious path bending left but take the fainter path bearing slightly right. Follow this as it veers right towards the left-hand edge of Princes Risborough, seen below. Cross the stile and continue on down until you meet a broad path. This is the Upper Icknield Way.

7. Turn left and go along it to a road. Turn right down the road and at the roundabout turn left. The tea shop is about 200 yards along on the left.

Princes Risborough is an ancient market town which has more modern housing estates than many would like: so much so that John Betjeman called it "untidy Metroland beneath the Chilterns". Be that as it may, the old centre down the High Street on the left has some attractive buildings. The seventeenth century Manor House was given to the National Trust by the Rothschild family in 1925 and is occasionally open to the public. It was used to store pictures from the National Gallery during the Second World War.

Princes Risborough was once known as Great Risborough. The royal connotation comes from the Black Prince who had a castle here. Today there are scant remains near the church.

8. Return to the roundabout and turn right back up New Road. After 75 yards turn left on a signed public footpath. Follow this as it crosses a road and then, when the houses end, across a field with a clear view of Whiteleaf Cross.

9. Turn left at a cross path. This is the Upper Icknield Way again. At a road (Peters Lane) turn left and walk down to the A4010.

10. Turn **LEFT**. Go along the service road with cottages on the right for a few yards and turn right down Burton Lane. When the road turns right continue ahead on a broad grassy path into the churchyard. Go round to the rear of the church and bear right to the road.

The picturesque cottages and church are part of Monks Risborough, a small place originally separated by fields from its larger neighbour but now more or less joined by suburban development. From before the Norman conquest it was owned by the monks of Christ Church, Canterbury, hence its name. The ancient church contains many old and interesting objects and the usual guide available within contains a wealth of detail.

Cottages near Monks Risborough

Monks Risborough, originally known as East Risborough, has the distinction of having the earliest confirmed Parish boundaries in England. The Risborough Charter dates from 903 though the existing document is a late tenth century copy which authorised one Aethelfrith to reproduce his lost land books from memory. The landmarks which marked the bounds can still be traced on the ground. They include some hedges still there today. Generally the age of a hedge can be judged from the number of species it contains: the more species, the older the hedge. Species counts suggest these boundary hedges are very ancient.

11. Take a signed public footpath directly opposite to a stile and a bridge over a small stream. A faint path goes to a fence on the left of the field. Do NOT follow this but cross a stile in the far left-hand corner of the field and then go across two small fields. The path then bears left and at a clearly marked path junction turn left to emerge on a road after about 50 yards.

12. Turn right through the village of Askett. At the main road turn right for 20 yards past The Three Crowns and then turn left on a signed public footpath. Walk along the right-hand side of five fields.

Askett is a straggling village with no real centre but some pretty cottages. Its lack of focus is proved by the fact that one lane is called Letter Box Lane!

13. At the far end of the fifth field the path joins the North Bucks Way. Cross an unwieldy double stile and go slightly right to a stile in a fence at the far side of the field as indicated by the North Bucks Way signs. Do NOT take the more obvious path which is at right angles towards farm buildings on the right. Go ahead by a summer house and over a drive to another stile and continue across a field to yet another stile.

14. Over this stile, fork right, following the North Bucks Way signs, to a metal kissing gate onto the A4010. The starting point is across the road.

17. Great Missenden and Wendover

Route: This is an exhilarating linear walk between Great Missenden and Wendover, two typical Chiltern towns. The return is made by train over an attractive part of the Chilterns line. There are trains every 30 minutes in the week and hourly at the weekends.

Tea shop: Le Bistro in Wendover is a French restaurant which none the less serves excellent English teas. The cream tea includes a toasted tea-cake with scones and cream. There are seats outside in summer opposite some pretty cottages but they are on a rather busy corner. Tel: 0296 622092

Distance: $5^1/_2$ miles.

Map: Landranger OS 165 Aylesbury and Leighton Buzzard.

How to get there: Great Missenden is just off the A413 Amersham – Aylesbury road. From the A413 take the A4128 High Wycombe road into Great Missenden and follow the signs to the station where there is a large car park. This is free at the weekends.

Start: Outside Great Missenden station. SP 893012

1. Turn left to the road and then right past some shops to a mini roundabout. Turn left and then right into Walnut Close. Continue in the same direction on a path at the end. This goes past a car park on the right.

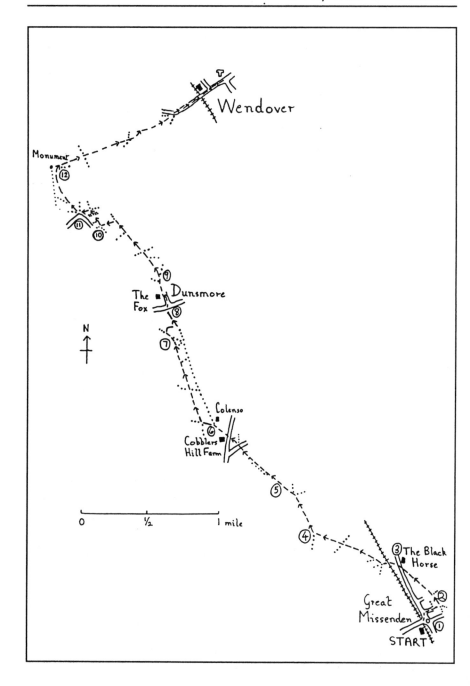

Great Missenden High Street was once part of the coach road to London and has many seventeenth and eighteenth century buildings.

Great Missenden once had a great abbey, the largest in Buckinghamshire. It was founded by William de Missenden in 1133 and had quite a scandalous history. Hugh de Plessetis, lord of the manor in the thirteenth century, was buried in the church yard together with his white palfrey Principal, his armour and the horse's harness. In 1297 a novice cut his throat "for fear of discipline" and one of the abbots was hanged for clipping the coins of Edward III! In 1530 there was another scandal when Abbot John Fox faced heavy charges against his community, one of whom "had been seen more than once coming out of a house in the village in doublet and jerkin with a sword by his side".

The abbey fell prey to the Dissolution in 1534 and the last abbot, John Otwell, accepted the inevitable and returned to secular life with a pension of £50 a year. The decayed estate was bought by James Oldham, a London ironmonger, in 1787 who built the building we see today. It incorporates a few traces of the original monastery. It is now used as a residential study centre by the county council.

Our route does not pass the abbey but it can clearly be seen on looking back towards the town.

2. Cross a stile and turn left. Cross another stile and continue in the same direction, ignoring a path over a stile to the right. After a while the path on the ground fades out. Continue in the same direction across the middle of the field heading to a stile by the third large tree from the right. The field you now enter is used as a caravan park and for balloon rallies. Cross to the road at The Black Horse.

You are now walking up the valley of the Misbourne which apparently rises in a pond we shall pass and flows fourteen miles southeast to the Coln near Uxbridge. History records that it has changed its course more than once, each change being said to presage a national disaster! The river is a poor thing today, dry in parts and in others no more than a trickle. Its name – a combination of the British "maes" or field and the Saxon "bourne", a river – is particularly appropriate for a river whose course is often marked just by a grass grown dip in the field, as you see to your left. In 1774 it was recorded as being 30 feet wide! It had a reputation for quirkiness even then. Old accounts tell of it running dry in wet winters and being in spate in times of drought.

A book issued by the Chiltern Society in 1987 called To Rescue a River *blames the present sad state of the river on over abstraction. Such a fuss has been made about this that efforts are being made to correct it but much of the river is still dry.*

3. Cross the road and turn right for 40 yards to a signed footpath on the left. Go straight ahead and under the railway. (*The pond on the left, which may be dried up, is said to be the source of the Misbourne. It has had much work done on it by the Chiltern Society.*)

   Over the stile the path bears right. After about 100 yards ignore a faint left branch but continue ahead to a stile. Cross the field diagonally on a very well defined path to some steps at the far end. At the top of the steps turn left and follow the field edge round. At the top of the field continue on the path into a wood.

4. Turn right at a T-junction at the end of the wood. Follow the path along the left-hand side of a field. Ahead right is an excellent view of Wendover Woods which is the highest point of the Chilterns. At the far side of the field continue on into a wood, ignoring a branch on the right. Just inside the wood the path forks. Take the left fork.

5. At the end of the wood continue on a path between hedges. This may sometimes be very muddy. If so, it can be avoided by taking a parallel path in the fields on the left. Cross a track and then the road at Cobblers Hill Farm and continue in the same direction. In 150 yards the track ends at a house called Colenso.

6. Take the stile on the left and cut across the corner of the small field to another stile. Cross this and go half left across the field to a stile part way along the fence opposite. Cross the stile. After 75 yards turn right along a crossing path. Follow this as it contours along the hill side with magnificent views on the left for about $1/2$ a mile. Ignore a crossing path after $1/4$ mile and two right turns.

7. The path comes to a stile. Cross this and turn left. After 75 yards, just before the main path bears left and starts to go downhill, take a faint path on the right. Do NOT go downhill. Follow this path round to the right and gently uphill to a track. Turn left.

8. Cross the road and continue down the road opposite into Dunsmore. Carry on past The Fox as the road deteriorates into a track. Ignore the first public footpath on the left but take the second after another 100 yards.

View across the Hampden Valley near Dunsmore

9. This path goes between wire fences and there are several side turns and cross paths. The fence on the right soon becomes a tall deer fence. Watch for a gate and cattle grid in this fence at a junction with a broad bridleway on the left. Carry on by the deer fence for a further 170 yards and then turn left. The junction is marked by yellow arrows on a tree.

10. After 200 yards turn right on a cross path marked with yellow arrows. Ignore several unmarked side turns and cross paths and continue until you come to a cross path where the left turn is marked by yellow arrows. Take this path and follow the arrows through an area of beech to a small car park.

11. Cross the car park to a wooden gate and take the centre one of three paths. When it divides, take the right fork to the monument on Coombe Hill.

Coombe Hill is the highest view point of the Chilterns but it is not the highest point. That lies 3 miles away in Wendover Woods. There are excellent views over the Vale of Aylesbury and it is said that you can see St. Paul's Cathedral but I doubt it. The monument is to 148 soldiers who died in the Boer War. The original metal plaque was stolen so now the names are engraved in the stone. The chalk grassland, heath and wood are included in a Site of Special Scientific Interest.

12. From the monument follow the Ridgeway to Wendover. There is a post with the Ridgeway symbol – a white acorn – to the right of the monument. At this point two paths apparently start! The Ridgeway is the lower of these. For more information about the Ridgeway see page 4. It goes downhill to a road. Turn right to carry on in the same direction into the town, passing the station on the left. Le Bistro is about 200 yards further on the left.

Wendover is a very ancient town first mentioned in 970 when the Saxon name Waendofran was used. However, it is certainly older than that: it is in an important gap in the hills, the Wendover Gap, which needed to be guarded as the many iron age hill forts in the vicinity prove.

On the High Street is the Manor Waste, Wendover's equivalent of a village green. Much damage was being done to it by indiscriminate car parking and so the council paved it with slabs and cobbles, planted trees and provided seats. Wendover has two fairs a year on the site, one in Spring and one in Autumn. Their charter dates back to 1214. The market on the Waste, on Thursday, has recently been reinstated. This is based on a fourteenth century charter which had lapsed for a great many years.

The borough returned two burgesses to Parliament in the early fourteenth century but allowed this privilege to lapse until 1625. It was then the smallest borough in England but had a remarkably distinguished list of representatives including, at different times, Edmund Burke, George Canning and John Hampden. In nearby Great Kimble church is a framed copy of the report of parish overseers setting out the names of those who refused to pay ship money. It is headed by John Hampden and his subsequent arrest and trial was one of the causes of the Civil War. He was related to Oliver Cromwell and fatally wounded on Chalgrove Field in 1643. Wendover was for many years the pocket borough of the Earls Verney and corruption was rife until the Reform Act.

18. Tring and The Ridgeway

Route: This walk starts by following The Ridgeway, the oldest path in Europe, and then drops down into the attractive old town of Tring. It returns via Tring Park.

Tea shop: Foxy's Corner House in Tring is a traditional tea shop with some tables outside in summer. It is open 10.30am until 5pm Monday to Saturday except Wednesday when it closes at 2pm. It is closed on Sunday. Tel: 0442 825350

Distance: 4 miles.

Map: Landranger OS 165 Aylesbury and Leighton Buzzard.

How to get there: From the A41, Tring bypass, follow the signs to Wigginton. Turn right down Chesham Road at the war memorial and then right along Wick Road opposite the Baptist chapel just before the Greyhound on the right. Go right to the end where there are several parking spots.

Start: At the end of Wick Road, Wigginton
               SP 936099

It is difficult to believe that this peaceful village was once known as "Wicked Wigginton".

It was renowned for its liberal publicans who were said never to turn a customer away regardless of licensing hours and cockfights were popular long after they were banned.

1. Walk along the track which is the continuation of Wick Road. After a few yards the Ridgeway path joins on the right.

Continue past Wick Farm for about $3/4$ of a mile to a road. Cross the road and continue in the same direction along Church Lane, signed Hastoe.

This is part of the Ridgeway path. For more information see page 4.

The Ridgeway Path

2. At the T-junction turn left along Gadmore lane and then immediately right on a signed public bridleway.

3. As the track approaches a house (Hastoe Grove) bear right through a wooden gate. Immediately after the gate take the path straight ahead signed Hastoe and Park Road, Tring. Do

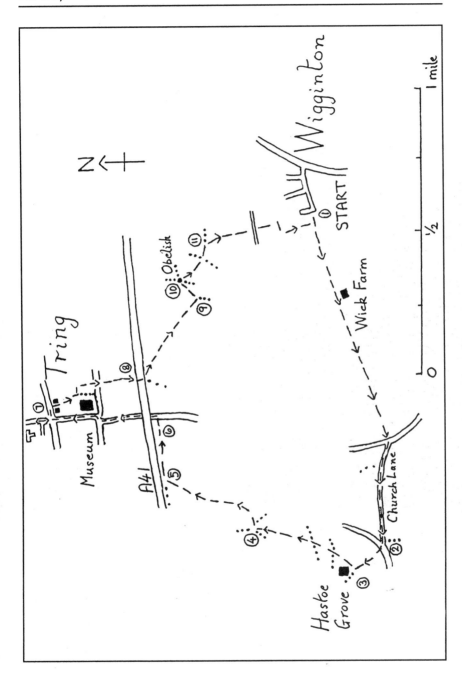

NOT turn right, signed Hastoe Hill. Follow this path downhill to a gate, ignoring all side turnings.

4. Do not go through the gate but turn right on a signed footpath just inside the wood.

5. At a T-junction in front of the bypass turn right. The path enters a field and continues along the left-hand side of this field and two further fields to a short stretch of surfaced track and the road.

6. Turn left and then at a T-junction turn right and follow the road round as it bends left past the Zoological Museum. Cross the High Street and continue in the same direction for a few yards to the tea shop.

Tring lies on Akeman Street, the Roman road from St. Albans to Aylesbury and the West. It was granted market rights by Edward II and another charter by Charles II. This prescribed that straw plait be sold in the mornings and corn in the afternoons.

Straw plaiting for straw hats was an important industry in many parts of the Chilterns. The straw needed to be narrow and soft and the thin Chilterns soils produced suitable raw material in abundance. It employed large numbers of women and children as a cottage industry and they could earn good money. How much they earned depended on how fast they worked but their wages compared well with those of agricultural labourers. This gave the women an unusual degree of independence which was not well received by everyone. The women were accused of being slovenly housewives and, more damming yet, to have a partiality to pretty clothes and loose morals. There is little evidence to substantiate this but it is true that female literacy lagged behind the rest of the country. This is because they went to school to learn their craft rather than the three Rs. The industry went into rapid decline after 1870 due to competition from cheap Chinese straw plait. The workers went into much more poorly paid work on the land or joined the drift to the cities.

Tring is best known today for its zoological museum. In 1872 the Rothschilds bought Tring Mansion. The Rothschilds were well known for their generosity to the town until the estate was sold in 1938. Walter Rothschild was an enthusiastic zoologist and in 1892 he opened the doors of his museum to the public providing an opportunity to see the greatest and most diverse animal collection ever made by one man. Lord Rothschild was particularly fascinated by big animals and the collection includes examples of the Komodo dragon (the largest living lizard) and the extinct giant moa among its thousands of exhibits ranging from the most commonplace to the rare and bizarre. When Walter Rothschild died in 1937 the museum was bequeathed to the Natural History Museum and is now an international centre for ornithological research. It is well worth a visit if you have time and is open Monday to Saturday 10.00 to 17.00 and Sunday 14.00 to 17.00. (Tel: 044 282 4181).

7. Return to the High Street and turn left. Turn right up an alley between the Midland and Nat West bank buildings. At the T-junction turn left. Cross the road and continue in the same direction on a path signed Tring park and Wigginton.

8. Cross the bypass by the footbridge and take the path on the left. This leads down into a dip and up the other side towards a wood.

This is Tring Park. If you look behind you can see the house which was built in the reign of Charles II but now has a Victorian facade. It was bought by the Rothschilds in 1872 and Walter Rothschild stocked the estate with various exotic animals such as kangaroos and cassowaries. Zebras were used to pull coaches. In those days the dangers of introducing exotic species were not so well appreciated as they are now. The edible dormouse, Glis glis, escaped and is spreading through the Chilterns and is something of a threat to the native dormouse because it is bigger and competes successfully for food. When the estate was sold, Hertfordshire County Council bought large areas of woodland to preserve them for public enjoyment.

9. Immediately after entering the wood bear left over a stile by a metal gate and follow the path up to the obelisk.

    The obelisk bears no inscription but is locally known as Nell Gwynn's Monument because she is supposed to have stayed in the Mansion and walked this way.

10. There are two paths on the right here. Of the two, take the one on the left which goes uphill more steeply. At the top cross a wide path to continue in the same direction.

11. Go through a gate and then turn right over a stile. You are now back on the Ridgeway. Stay on the Ridgeway path, crossing a drive, to the track along which the walk started. Turn left for a few yards back to the starting point.

19. *Aldbury and The Grand Union Canal*

Route: This walk starts along the bank of the Grand Union canal and returns by Aldbury. Aldbury is a picture postcard village, complete with pond, stocks and tea shop and can be busy but apart from that the paths are not well used and the route is very quiet.

Tea shop: Town Farm Tea Room is in the middle of the village, tucked away behind the main street. It is in a well designed modern building in a lovely setting. There are seats outside under a pergola. It offers a range of teas including a farm house tea with a boiled egg! The tea rooms are open every day but Monday and Friday and every bank holiday except Christmas Day.
Tel: 0442 85239

Distance: 4 miles.

Map: Landranger OS 165 Aylesbury and Leighton Buzzard.

How to get there: Tring station is not in Tring town but about 2 miles east. It is signed from the A4251 and from the town.

Start: Tring Station where there is a very large car park.
SP 951122

---

1. From the car park turn left along the road over the railway, past the Royal Hotel and houses, to the canal.

   The Grand Union canal here is a great feat of Victorian engineering. It passes through Tring Gap which has always been a natural route through the Chilterns and so attracted monumental engineering works from the Romans onwards.The canal was originally called the Grand Junction Canal and was part of a scheme to link the Trent with the Thames so coal and other cargoes could be transported economically to London from the Midlands and the North. It was built by William Jessop who constructed a series of locks to take boats up and over the Chilterns. However, evry time the lock gates are opened some water is lost. In the dry Chilterns there is no natural source for replenishment. The solution was to build a number of reservoirs near Tring from which water could be pumped up into the canal. These are now nature reserves famous for the variety of bird life they attract.

The heyday of the canals did not last long before they were supplanted by the railways. The railway cutting dug out north of Tring Station was also considered one of the great engineering works of the age: one and a half million tons of earth were shifted by men and horses.

2. Turn right down some steps and left along the tow path. Walk along the tow-path for $1^1/_2$ miles to the second bridge, number 137, at Cowroast Lock.

   Cowroast Lock is not, as might be imagined, the site of some gigantic barbecue but is a corruption of the term Cow Rest. This was a favourite resting place of drovers as they took cattle through the hills to the London markets.

3. Turn left along the lane for 200 yards and then take a stile, quite well hidden in the hedge, on the left. Follow the path across the field and footbridge over the railway and then straight ahead across another field to a fenced track.

4. Turn right and follow the track round past a farm to a T-junction with another track. Turn left into the farm yard and immediately right to a stile by a metal gate. The path then goes half left diagonally across the field to a stile by a metal gate in the top left-hand corner.

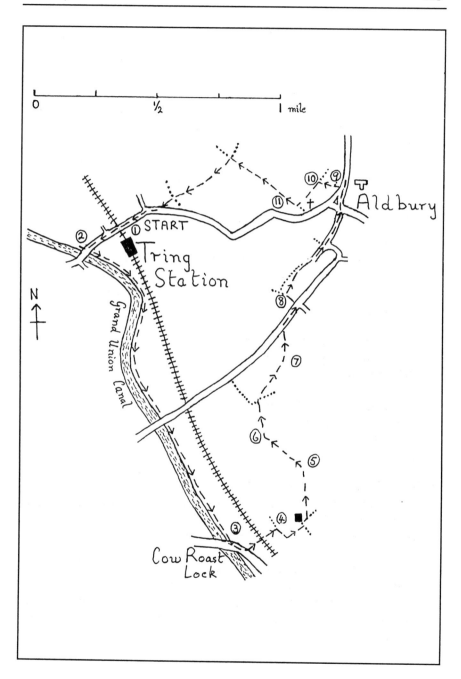

5. Over the stile walk towards the near left-hand edge of a hedge seen ahead and then continue in the same direction with the hedge on the right. In the corner go through a hedge gap and through a narrow strip of scrub up to a stile.

6. The path is not visible on the ground but goes half left uphill to the top left-hand corner of the field and a stile. It then follows the edge of the wood round to the right, crossing a signed bridleway. Over a stile by a metal gate the path is more obvious and continues just inside the wood to another stile.

7. Bear half left across the field to a stile. Walk along the right-hand side of the field for a few yards to a stile on the right and then across the corner of a third small field to the road. Turn right for 200 yards to a public bridleway on the left.

Ahead and right, on top of the hill, can be seen the Bridgewater Monument. This is visited on walk 20, see page 130.

8. After 120 yards cross a stile on the right and walk along the left-hand side of the field towards Aldbury seen ahead. At the far side continue ahead to the road and carry on in the same direction along the road into the centre of the village. The tea shop is at the far end of the pond, opposite the Greyhound.

Aldbury hugs the base of the Chiltern escarpment. It must be one of the most visited and photographed Chiltern villages. It has all the necessary ingredients – a wealth of old and charming buildings in a great variety of styles, a large pond well supplied with ducks and a village green complete with stocks and whipping post. These reminders of a more brutal past were once found on every village green and used to punish crimes such as playing games on Sunday as well as more serious offences.

The stocks gave their name to a house just outside the village which was the home of Mrs Humphrey Ward. She was a Victorian novelist who wrote highly sentimental books not much read today. Her novel "Bessie Costrell" is set in Clinton Magna, otherwise Aldbury. She entertained many other eminent Victorians such as Henry James and Bernard Shaw and was aunt to Julian and Aldous Huxley who spent many happy days at Stocks. She was the first woman magistrate in Britain.

Aldbury

9. From the tea room cross the road and take the drive to the left of the Greyhound. At the end of the drive cross a stile on the right into a playing field and go up the left-hand side to another stile.

10. Turn left and walk round the edge of the field, passing the church on the left. Next to a barn the right of way crosses a stile to go on a very overgrown path between the barn and the hedge which leads into a tiny triangular field. Most people continue along the edge of the field to a gate on the left into this little field.

11.Cross the stile and continue on the fenced path to another stile.
   Turn left on a cross path and continue along this until it joins
   the Ridgeway (see page 4). Carry on in the same direction and
   after about 50 yards join a surfaced drive to the road. Turn
   right back to the starting point.

20. Ashridge Estate

Route: The Ashridge Estate, owned by the National Trust, comprises some 4000 acres of commons and woods freely open to the public. This short level walk offers excellent views for remarkably little effort.

Tea shop: Teas are served next to the information centre on summer weekends and during the week (except Friday) in August from 2pm to 5.30pm.
Tel: 044 285 227.

Distance: 2 miles.

Map: Landranger OS 165 Aylesbury and Leighton Buzzard.

How to get there: Take the B4506 from the A41 at Northchurch, 1 mile NW of Berkhamsted. After 3 miles turn left on a surfaced road which is the entrance to the estate. Park as close as possible to the entrance.

Start: At the entrance to the estate.
SP 979128

Ashridge House, which can be glimpsed through the trees from the entrance, is the latest of several buildings on this site. Richard Earl of Cornwall, Henry III's brother brought back from the crusades a golden box containing what was said to be the blood of Christ. In 1276 Richard's son Edmund founded a monastery here. For 250 years the monastery was a site of pilgrimage and received many rich offerings. It is said to have been connected to a nearby nunnery by a secret passage but perhaps that is just Dissolution gossip!

In 1539 Henry VIII suppressed the monastery and showed the relic to be a fake. It became a home for his children and the future Elizabeth I was staying there in 1554 when she was arrested on suspicion of being involved in a plot to remove Mary from the throne.

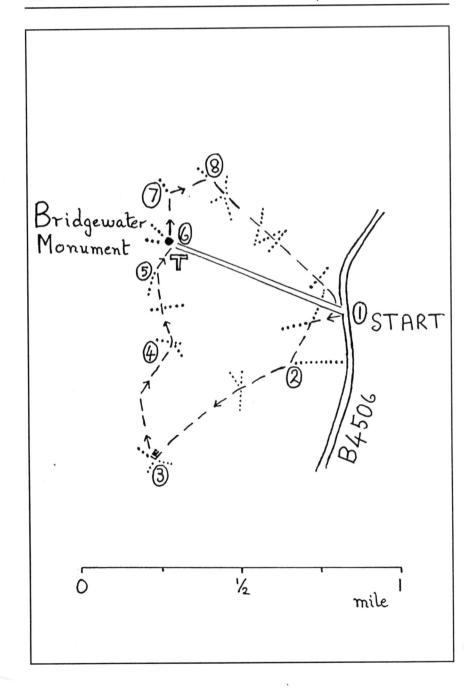

The present building was started at the beginning of the nineteenth century and took ten years to complete. It was designed by James Wyatt, known as "The Destroyer" for his works on various English cathedrals. Views on the house vary: some have considered it a monstrosity while others have called it spectacular but is certainly a classic example of Gothic revival. It is not owned by the National Trust and today is a well known management college. It is open to the public on a few days a year.

1. Turn right along the B4506 for 30 yards and turn right on an unsigned path into the woods. After 180 yards turn left along a very narrow crossing path. This is easy to miss. At the time of writing there is a "No Horses" sign in green on a tree a few yards down the path.

2. Just before the wood ends, turn right on a broader path at a T-junction. In less than $1/4$ mile you will reach a crossing path followed immediately by a split in the path. Take the left fork to continue on the same path to a wooden gate by a house.

The Ashridge Estate came into the hands of the Egerton family in 1604 and there it remained until 1921 when the will of the final private owner decreed it was to be sold. Up until then people in the area had enjoyed the freedom of this beautiful estate but that soon changed as the trustees set about disposing of the estate piecemeal. Many mature trees were felled and sold for timber. Fortunately, some influential people were appalled. The prominent historian Professor G.M. Trevelyan approached the National Trust. At the same time a Miss Bridget Talbot, a cousin of the Egerton family,approached the Prime Minister, Stanley Baldwin. He, together with the leaders of the other two parties and the National Trust appealed to the public to raise the money and to the trustees for time. These petitions brought an outstanding response, especially among local people, and enabled the National Trust to buy 1,700 acres immediately and other parcels of land at intervals since.

3. Turn right. 5 yards after the end of the garden fence, branch

right on a path between two holly bushes. This is parallel to the bridle way which can be very muddy and cut up. Ignore all side paths and continue on the main path. It eventually veers slightly right and uphill away from the bridleway.

4. At the top of the hill ignore paths right and left to continue in the wood with an open area close by on the right. The Bridgewater Monument and tea room soon come into view.

The Bridgewater Monument

5. At a T-junction with a wider path turn right to the monument and tea room. Next to the shop and tea room is a museum display about the history and management of the estate.

In 1748, at the age of 11, Francis Egerton became the 3rd Duke of Bridgewater. He grew up to be a man of enormous body and not a little eccentricity. He swore he would never again speak to a woman after his fiancee broke off their engagement and he kept his word as far as is known. His fame today rests on his collaboration with an illiterate but inspired engineer called James Brindley. One supplied the cash and the other the knowhow to build the first entirely artificial canal in Britain. Its purpose was to carry coal from the Duke's mines at Worsley into Manchester. It cut the price of coal in the city by half and inspired a transport revolution.

A later Francis Egerton left £13,500 for a monument to be built to his own design commemorating his illustrious ancestor. Lady Bridgewater thought the design in poor taste and had it built well away from the house. It is 108 feet high and has 172 steps. It is open some days in the summer and if you have stamina to climb up you will be rewarded with fine views of the surrounding countryside.

6. From the monument take the bridleway signed Nature Trail.

7. After 300 yards turn right on a broad bridleway.

   Ashridge Estate encompasses most of the habitats to be found in the Chilterns; mature woodland, scrub, chalk grassland and farmed land. This walk is mainly through woodland areas known as Old Copse and Aldbury Common but an exploration of the rest of the estate is highly recommended.

   Aldbury Common is the only one at Ashridge where the ancient right of commoners survive. Commons does not refer to ownership since commons are owned by an individual or an institution. It refers to the use of the land and are today, by definition, those lands where common rights have been registered under the Commons Act 1965. They include activities such as fern and furze cutting, removal of fallen wood and pasturing horses, cows, pigs and sheep. Today, of course, these rights are often not exercised.

8. After 200 yards turn right at a T-junction. At a complex junction after 200 yards continue in the same direction bearing only slightly left. Continue on the same path ignoring all side turnings and crossing paths back to the entrance.

If you enjoy walking 'on the level', be sure to read:

MOSTLY DOWNHILL, Leisurely Walks in the Lake District

MOSTLY DOWNHILL, Leisurely Walks in the White Peak

MOSTLY DOWNHILL, Leisurely Walks in the Dark Peak

Easy, enjoyable walking books; all £6.95

We publish a wide range of other titles, including general interest publications, guides to individual towns, and books for outdoor activities centred on walking and cycling in the great outdoors throughout England and Wales. This is a recent selection:

Cycling with Sigma ...

**CYCLE UK! The definitive guide to leisure cycling
– Les Lumsdon** *(£9.95)*

**OFF-BEAT CYCLING & MOUNTAIN BIKING IN THE PEAK DISTRICT
– Clive Smith** *(£6.95)*

**MORE OFF-BEAT CYCLING IN THE PEAK DISTRICT
– Clive Smith** *(£6.95)*

**50 BEST CYCLE RIDES IN CHESHIRE
– edited by Graham Beech** *(£7.95)*

**CYCLING IN THE LAKE DISTRICT
– John Wood** *(£7.95)*

**CYCLING IN SOUTH WALES
– Rosemary Evans** *(£7.95)*

**BY-WAY BIKING IN THE CHILTERNS
– Henry Tindell** *(£7.95)*

Books of Walks

There are many more books for outdoor people in our catalogue, including:

RAMBLES IN NORTH WALES
– Roger Redfern

HERITAGE WALKS IN THE PEAK DISTRICT
– Clive Price

EAST CHESHIRE WALKS
– Graham Beech

WEST CHESHIRE WALKS
– Jen Darling

WEST PENNINE WALKS
– Mike Cresswell

STAFFORDSHIRE WALKS
– Les Lumsdon

NEWARK AND SHERWOOD RAMBLES
– Malcolm McKenzie

NORTH NOTTINGHAMSHIRE RAMBLES
– MAlcolm McKenzie

RAMBLES AROUND NOTTINGHAM & DERBY
– Keith Taylor

RAMBLES AROUND MANCHESTER
– Mike Cresswell

WESTERN LAKELAND RAMBLES
– Gordon Brown

WELSH WALKS:
Dolgellau and the Cambrian Coast
– Laurence Main and Morag Perrott

WELSH WALKS:
Aberystwyth and District
– Laurence Main and Morag Perrott

MOSTLY DOWNHILL:
Leisurely walks in the Lake District
– Alan Pears

WEST PENNINE WALKS
– Mike Cresswell

– all of the above books are currently £6.95 each

CHALLENGING WALKS IN NORTH-WEST BRITAIN
– Ron Astley *(£9.95)*

WALKING PEAKLAND TRACKWAYS
– Mike Cresswell *(£7.95)*

The Best Pub Walks!

Sigma publish the widest range of "Pub Walks" guides, covering just about every popular walking destination in England and Wales. Each book includes 25 – 30 interesting walks and varied suitable for individuals or family groups. *The walks are based on "Real Ale" inns of character and are all accessible by public transport.*

Areas covered include

Cheshire • Dartmoor • Exmoor • Isle of Wight • Yorkshire Dales • Peak District • Lake District • Cotswolds • Mendips • Cornwall • Lancashire • Oxfordshire • Snowdonia • Devon

… and dozens more – all £6.95 each!

General interest:

THE INCREDIBLY BIASED BEER GUIDE – Ruth Herman
This is the most comprehensive guide to Britain's smaller breweries and the pubs where you can sample their products. Produced with the collaboration of the Small Independent Brewers' Association and including a half-price subscription to The Beer Lovers' Club. *£6.95*

DIAL 999 – EMERGENCY SERVICES IN ACTION – John Creighton
Re-live the excitement as fire engines rush to disasters. See dramatic rescues on land and sea. Read how the professionals keep a clear head and swing into action. *£9.95*

THE ALABAMA AFFAIR – David Hollett
This is an account of Britain's role in the American Civil War. Read how Merseyside dockyards supplied ships for the Confederate navy, thereby supporting the slave trade. The *Alabama* was the most famous of the 'Laird Rams', and was chased half way across the world before being sunk ignominiously. *£9.95*

PEAK DISTRICT DIARY – Roger Redfern
An evocative book, celebrating the glorious countryside of the Peak District. The book is based on Roger's popular column in *The Guardian* newspaper and is profusely illustrated with stunning photographs. *£6.95*

I REMAIN, YOUR SON JACK – J. C. Morten (edited by Sheila Morten)
A collection of almost 200 letters, as featured on BBC TV, telling the moving story of a young soldier in the First World War. Profusely illustrated with contemporary photographs. *£8.95*